Living Free
Participant's Guide
Second Edition
By Jimmy Ray Lee, D. Min. and Dan Strickland, M.Div.

Communications should be addressed to:
Living Free®
P.O. Box 22127
Chattanooga, TN 37422-2127

Unless otherwise indicated, all Scripture quotations are taken from the *Holy Bible,* New International Version®. NIV®. Copyright © 1973, 1978, 1984 by International Bible Society. Used by permission of Zondervan Publishing House. All rights reserved.

Scripture quotations marked NKJV are taken from the New King James Version. Copyright © 1979, 1980, 1982 by Thomas Nelson, Inc. Used by permission. All rights reserved.

Scripture verses marked Phillips are taken from *The New Testament in Modern English* by J. B. Phillips, copyright © J. B. Phillips, 1958, 1959, 1960, 1972. All rights reserved.

Scripture quotations marked AMP are taken from *The Amplified Bible*. Old Testament copyright © 1965, 1987 by The Zondervan Corporation. *The Amplified New Testament* Copyright © 1958, 1987 by The Lockman Foundation. Used by permission.

Scripture quotations marked TLB are taken from *The Living Bible* copyright © 1971. Used by permission of Tyndale House Publishers, Inc., Wheaton, Illinois 60189. All rights reserved.

Scripture quotations marked NLT are taken from *The Holy Bible, New Living Translation,* copyright © 1996. Used by permission of Tyndale House Publishers, Inc., Wheaton, Illinois 60189. All rights reserved.

Extracts from *Understanding the Times and Knowing What to Do* are reproduced by permission of Living Free®

Copyright © 1999, 2008 by Living Free®. All rights reserved.

Living Free, and the Living Free logos are trademarks of Living Free®.

Updated 2017

All rights are reserved. No part of the material protected by this copyright notice may be reproduced or utilized in any form or by any means, electronic or mechanical, including photocopying, recording, or any information storage and retrieval system, without written permission from Living Free®.

Living Free.
Discovering God's Path to Freedom

Cover Graphic by Linda Miller
Arnold Miller Promotions

Layout by Louise Lee

The authors wish to thank the following contributing writers and editors:
 Nancy Ryken Taylor
David Schmidt
Jan Sokoloski
Lucinda Armas

About the Authors

Dr. Jimmy Ray Lee is the founder and president of Living Free®. He is the author of *Understanding the Times* and several small group studies published by Living Free®.

Dr. Lee is the founder and honorary chairman of Project 714 (now known as National Center for Youth Issues), a chemical prevention/intervention program for schools. He also founded an inner-city ministry called Ark Ministries that reached 600 to 700 young people weekly. He started the Chattanooga Teen Challenge and served as its president for three years. Jimmy served as Nashville Teen Challenge executive director during its formative years.

In 1983 he was awarded the "Service to Mankind Award" presented by the Highland Sertoma Club in Hixson, Tennessee.

Dan Strickland has served as Vice President of Living Free® for over 16 years. As well as participating in the day-to-day operation of the ministry, he trains churches in the U.S. and internationally to implement Living Free® groups. Prior to joining Living Free®, he served as adult pastor and counselor in the First Assembly of God Church, Memphis, Tennessee, where Living Free® groups involved hundreds of participants in the congregation and community. Dan is a graduate of Central Bible College, and he earned the Master of Divinity degree from Southwestern Baptist Theological Seminary.

Living Free video training is produced by IMS Productions, in consultation with J. David Schmidt & Associates.

Participant's Guide: Living Free DVD Training, Living Free®, P. O. Box 22127, Chattanooga, TN 37422-2127

Living Free DVD Training

Table of Contents

Participant's Guide

Living Free Ministry Overview	1
Living Free Training Summary	4

Part 1: Learning to Live Free

Segment 1: Defining Life-Controlling Problems	7
Segment 2: Mastered and Trapped by Issues	14
Segment 3: Walls of Protection	23
Segment 4: Family Influences	32
Segment 5: Helping or Harming?	41

Part 2: Helping Others to Live Free through Small Groups

Segment 6: The Small Group Strategy	52
Segment 7: Effective Facilitation and Communication	59
Segment 8: Launching a Living Free Ministry	71

Appendices

Knowing More	80
Plan of Salvation	98
References	99

Participant's Guide: Living Free DVD Training, Living Free®, P. O. Box 22127, Chattanooga, TN 37422-2127

Participant's Guide: Living Free DVD Training, Living Free®, P. O. Box 22127, Chattanooga, TN 37422-2127

Living Free Ministry Overview

Equipping local churches to help people prevent and overcome life-controlling problems.

Behind People's Sunday Smiles Is a World of Hurt

Most people sit in church with smiles on their faces.

Some of these "Sunday" smiles hide painful struggles. Depression. Overwork. Anger. Emotional numbness. An unhealthy relationship or an adulterous affair. Dependency on alcohol, drugs, or people's approval. From eating disorders to sexual addiction, there are people in your church who are struggling with life-controlling problems. They don't experience freedom and full life in Christ. Instead, they find themselves trapped. Some want help. Others don't. For those who want help but are afraid to ask, where do they go?

HERE ARE ANSWERS TO A FEW QUESTIONS YOU MAY HAVE ABOUT LIVING FREE.

What Is Living Free?

Living Free is a nonprofit Christian ministry with a mission to help your church reach out to people facing life-controlling problems, hurts, and the everyday challenges of life that can become overwhelming. This unique program uses lay leadership, small groups, and Bible studies on a wide variety of topics. The Bible studies are specifically designed to help group members deal honestly with real-life problems.

Living Free is not a Christian 12-step program. It is not pop-psychology. Nor can it replace the work of a trained counselor when one is needed. Rather, it shows how your church or ministry can bring together the *Word of God*, the *Spirit of God*, and the *People of God* to help others break free from and remain free of life-controlling problems.

Since its founding by Dr. Jimmy Ray Lee in 1988, thousands of churches, ministries, and individuals in a wide variety of settings have used Living Free materials. Our reach has expanded internationally, with resources in several languages. Wherever we minister, we work in cooperation with churches to offer a model for setting up and running small groups that help people grow to their full potential in Christ.

The Living Free model is implemented by a team of church members under the supervision of your church leadership. Living Free provides this DVD series for training facilitators (or leaders) of small groups, as well as curriculum to be used in follow-up groups. Your Living Free training coordinator has a current list of available curriculum.

What Benefits Does Living Free Offer My Church?

We live in a society that is full of people who choose to live self-destructive lifestyles. Our communities and our churches are filled with hurting people who are looking for answers. Many times church does not feel like a safe place for people who need to talk about their struggles and find hope. Beginning this ministry in your church can provide opportunities for people to overcome those struggles in a Christ-centered small group.

A Word to Parachurch Ministries

Living Free works effectively in parachurch ministries, too. Youth programs, outreach organizations, and missionary agencies have established Living Free ministries to reach out to the people they serve. While throughout this training we refer to the local church, the Living Free content and small group methodology are applicable to other Christian ministries as well.

Jesus commissioned Paul to "open their eyes and turn them from darkness to light, and from the power of Satan to God, so that they may receive forgiveness of sins and a place among those who are sanctified by faith in me" (Acts 26:18).

At Living Free, we believe those instructions to Paul are our marching orders, too. Everything we do, from our training to our curriculum, focuses on helping people live freely in Jesus Christ.

How Would a Living Free Ministry Work in My Church?

YOU CAN START A LIVING FREE MINISTRY IN YOUR CHURCH BY TAKING FOUR SIMPLE STEPS:

1. **Offer this *Living Free* training to interested persons in your congregation.** The segments of this DVD series provide valuable information to people who want to learn more about preventing and overcoming life-controlling problems. They are especially helpful in surfacing and training potential Living Free group facilitators.

2. **Form a Core Team.** After the training, facilitators and other interested lay leaders will work as a team (we call it a Core Team) to develop small groups that address life-controlling issues. Segment 8 of this training walks you through the Core Team concept and the steps to implementing a Living Free ministry in your church.

3. **Have the Core Team participate in an *Insight Group*.** Upon completion of the *Insight Group*, facilitators will invite others to participate in the *Insight Group* and subsequent groups.

4. **Establish groups that meet people at their point of need.** The *Insight Group* should be the first group offered. As mentioned earlier, your training coordinator has a current catalog listing our curriculum. With a Core Team established and small groups up and running, Living Free will become an ongoing ministry in your church to meet the specific needs of your congregation and community.

Your church may decide to use its own small group curriculum after the *Living Free* DVD training. We would still encourage you to go through the *Insight Group* first. This provides an excellent training ground for potential facilitators of small groups. In this group, new facilitators can experience and put into practice concepts and skills learned from the training.

If you have any questions about this training or about Living Free, please call us at 1.800.879.4770 or email info@LivingFree.org.

How It Works

Hold Living Free Training
Potential facilitators and interested persons participate in the *Living Free* training.

▼

Form a Core Team
Potential facilitators and lay leaders form a Core Team.

▼

Offer an *Insight Group*
Facilitators and Core Team members participate in an *Insight Group*. All other interested persons enroll in an *Insight Group*.

▼

Establish Small Groups
After the *Insight Group*, participants enroll in other small groups.

Living Free Training Summary

Discovering God's Path to Spiritual Freedom

OBJECTIVES OF THIS TRAINING

AT THE END OF THIS TRAINING, YOU WILL HAVE THE KNOWLEDGE AND PRACTICAL STRATEGIES NECESSARY TO BETTER:

1. Understand life-controlling issues—how they develop and the impact they have on individuals and families.

2. Prevent life-controlling problems or deal with them in your own life.

3. Help others with life-controlling issues. If you decide to become a facilitator of a Living Free small group, this training will help equip you to lead a small group effectively.

4. Establish an ongoing Living Free ministry.

Living Free was designed to benefit those who want to become facilitators of small groups and those who simply want to better understand life-controlling problems and how they affect one's walk with God.

If you are still deciding whether you should participate in the **Living Free** training, here's a quick self-test.

- Would you like to learn more about life-controlling problems?

- Does your heart go out to people who can't seem to break free from a damaging behavior, relationship, or substance?

- Are you struggling with a particular issue or problem that hinders your walk with God?

- Does someone you love have a life-controlling problem?

- Would you like to become a small group facilitator where there is caring, accountability, and confidentiality?

If you can answer yes to any one of these questions, then you are in the right place!

How Each Segment Is Organized

There are a total of eight segments in this DVD training series. Each segment of the *Participant's Guide* has the four sections listed below:

INTRODUCTION
A brief description of the DVD segment and a few items to look for as you watch it.

SELF-AWARENESS
A detailed outline of the key points and content covered in the DVD segment.

SPIRITUAL AWARENESS
Key Bible passages and insights from Scripture that relate to the material covered in this segment.

APPLICATION

- **TALK ABOUT IT**
  3-4 questions to discuss as a group that relate to the DVD you've just seen.

- **PERSONAL REFLECTION**
  Reflective exercises to do at home that will help participants process what was discussed in the session.

Helpful information that goes beyond what is covered in the video segment can be found in the back of the Coordinator's and Participant's Guides in a section called **KNOWING MORE**.

Use of *Living Free* Training Series

The *Living Free* training series is designed to work under the auspices of Living Free, Inc., its staff, and certified instructors. You are authorized to use the Living Free DVD training series in your congregation and/or parachurch ministry at your customary places of assembly. Any other use must be specifically authorized by Living Free. For authorization call 423.899.4770.

These restrictions are designed to protect the integrity of the content of the material and its intended purpose as designed by Living Free, Inc.

Here Is an Overview of What's Ahead in Each Segment:

In **Segments 1-5**, you will learn more about life-controlling problems—the main types of issues, how they develop, and their impact on individuals and entire families. This portion of the training is useful for future facilitators or any interested person.

Segments 6-7 focus on Living Free's small group strategy. In these segments you will discover how small groups can help people become free and remain free of life-controlling problems. You will also learn some essential skills of small group leadership. Potential facilitators should definitely be involved in these segments, but they are also useful for people who are interested in learning more about life-controlling problems and everyday life issues.

Segment 8 explains how to start a Living Free ministry in your church. It addresses those people who will be responsible for running the ministry. Facilitators should participate in Segment 8 so that they will understand and share in the process for managing the program.

It is our prayer at Living Free that this training might benefit you personally and also the people God brings into your life.

The DVD features actors who play characters with certain life-controlling problems. It also features people who tell about their real-life experiences with the same types of problems. These people who are not actors are identified by their first names on the screen (e.g., Candy, Joe, Brad . . .).

Segment 1: Defining Life-Controlling Problems

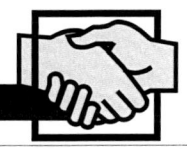

Introduction

Welcome to Living Free. You are about to begin an exciting journey of self-awareness and learning. We thank God for your participation.

DVD (13 Minutes)

As you watch the opening video, look for answers to these questions:

What is a life-controlling problem?

How can I recognize a life-controlling problem in myself or someone I love?

How might Living Free benefit me?

At the conclusion of the video, read the following pages for further information. Then consider the questions under Application.

Self-Awareness

What is a life-controlling problem?

"Everything is permissible for me—but I will not be mastered by anything" (I Corinthians 6:12).

Life-controlling problems are anything that master our lives and block our spiritual growth.

Other descriptions include: life-controlling struggle, addiction, dependency, stronghold, besetting sin, slavery, compulsive behavior.

A **life-controlling problem** is anything that stands in the way of our spiritual growth and relationship with God or brings us under its power.

- Life-controlling problems may be something that people consider positive—things like work, sports, or ministry—or they may be things that people consider negative, such as alcohol, drugs, gambling, or sexual addictions.

- We may become consumed with another person's problem and try to fix it, allowing their problem to enslave us as well.

- We may be trapped by emotions that overwhelm us—grief, depression, anger.

- Or life-controlling problems may be sinful attitudes and mindsets such as bitterness, envy, or lust.

Who struggles with life-controlling problems?

Nearly all people are dealing with some struggle in their lives.

Almost everyone has something blocking his or her spiritual growth in Christ.

The Bible refers to these things as strongholds.

A stronghold is an area of sin that has become part of our lifestyle. It may be a harmful habit (drugs, fornication, smoking), or it may be an attitude (rejection, loneliness, worry, doubt). We use a whole arsenal of rationalizations and speculations to support these habits or attitudes. But the knowledge on which these strongholds are based directly opposes God's truth (Stanley, 118).

Some strongholds are known only to ourselves, while others are obvious to everyone around us.

When we are trapped in these problems, we feel helpless. We want to change, but our failures discourage us. Some people quit trying and never grow beyond a certain point in their Christian journey.

The 20–60–20 ratio

People don't usually talk in church about the things that are bothering them under the surface, but people are struggling. One helpful thing to be aware of is the 20-60-20 ratio, which describes most congregations.

Life-controlling Problems and Addiction

Addiction and life-controlling problems have a common bond—they master a person.

An addiction is a state of compulsion, obsession, or preoccupation that enslaves desire and creates the state of dependency.

The word addicted has become generalized and is no longer confined to the World Health Organization's definition (which only describes addiction to drugs)… In other words, people are now seen to be "addicted" to different things as food, smoking, gambling, work, spending money, play, video games, sex, pleasing people and religion (Miller, 44).

"I have witnessed the sobering reality that addiction is stronger than human love. Powerful natural disasters like hurricanes or tornadoes do not compel fathers and mothers to abandon their children. But addiction does" (Hersh, 5).

Typically 20 percent of the congregation are the faithful supporters and active lay leaders.

Many are doing quite well, but some are secretly having a hard time. They feel that they must be the examples in the church and that admitting to a life-controlling issue would damage their testimony.

Even those who are doing well may have areas of life in which they keep getting trapped by something. Some will have friends and loved ones with life-controlling problems that affect their lives.

The middle 60 percent represents the majority of the congregation.

They seem to be doing okay, but many are hiding their struggles. Some individuals in this group may not be aware that they have a life-controlling issue, but they are in pain.

Many of these people may also be feeling the effects of someone else's problems.

The remaining 20 percent are those who struggle openly.

Unfortunately, this is the group that is most often labeled "those kinds of people." These are probably the people who came to mind when you first heard the words "life-controlling problem" or "addiction." They are openly dealing with issues like substance abuse or behavioral or relationship problems. Much pastoral care in the church is directed toward these people. Many people in this group were once part of the larger group—the 60 percent majority.

No one is immune to struggles or sin.

Because we all struggle, everyone has the potential for developing a life-controlling problem. As Hebrews 12:1-2 instructs us, sin will try to entangle us and prevent us from progressing in the Christian life. We have to resist the influence of sin as long as we live in mortal bodies, and we know from painful experience that everyone is vulnerable. To continue to grow in Christ requires that we continually look to the Lord for his help and inspiration.

Nobody thinks that allowing sinful habits to begin will lead to becoming mastered by sin, but it happens all the time. When we allow an area of sin to become part of how we live, we open the door to being mastered by that

---

Remember that some men's sins are obvious, and are equally obvious bringing them into judgment. The sins of other men are not apparent, but are dogging them, nevertheless, under the surface. Similarly some virtues are plain to see, while others, though not at all conspicuous, will eventually become known (1 Timothy 5:24-25, Phillips).

Therefore, since we are surrounded by such a huge crowd of witnesses to the life of faith, let us strip off every weight that slows us down, especially the sin that so easily trips us up. And let us run with endurance the race God has set before us. We do this by keeping our eyes on Jesus, the champion who initiates and perfects our faith. Because of the joy awaiting him, he endured the cross, disregarding its shame. Now he is seated in the place of honor beside God's throne (Hebrews 12:1-2, NLT).

sin. Instead of looking to Jesus for help and inspiration, we become distracted and focused on ourselves and on the sin that is entangling us.

These struggles can be described as addictions, dependencies, controlling behaviors, or even just the normal challenges of life that sometimes overwhelm us.

People fear being labeled.

We resist admitting our struggles because we fear what others think—so we hide our struggles behind smiles.

We fear being "labeled," or identified by our problems. Labels help summarize and describe behaviors, but when used unwisely, labeling is destructive and does not help anyone live free in Christ. All Christians struggle from time to time with certain issues, and labeling keeps us from finding a place where we can identify, confess, and overcome our struggles with sin.

Just as we don't want to be labeled, we should avoid labeling others.

That's where Living Free fits in. It provides a safe place for all of us to move to the next level of spiritual and personal growth, without fear of being labeled.

Whether you have a life-controlling problem yourself or live with someone who does, whether you are an experienced small group leader or have never been in a small group before, Living Free is for you. We can equip you and your church to provide small groups where participants may know that:

- They won't be labeled by problems they may have.
- They have the freedom to take off their masks and receive Christian love and support.
- They will be given practical steps to apply Scripture to daily life.

A World Health Organization study found that those countries that place such labels [as mental illness] on persons struggling with emotional stability, the recidivism rate (getting sick again) was much higher than in those countries where people were not labeled (Sweeten, 62).

Throughout this training you will learn more about how the program works and how you can help implement it in your church. For a brief summary, turn back to pages 1-6 in this workbook.

Living Free is based on 3 assumptions:
- The Bible is the final authority for daily living.
- The Holy Spirit is working today as our teacher, counselor, and guide.
- The community of believers are connected with each other and with God.

Spiritual Awareness Lead-In

Freedom from all these struggles is only found in Christ, and we come to know Him and experience His love for us in the pages of His Word, the Bible. Each group meeting will move from the video and Self-Awareness sections into what we call "Spiritual Awareness," which is a time of learning from God's Word.

Spiritual Awareness

Let's start by discussing why we should turn to God's Word.

Living Free is designed to help the average Christian find the resources to overcome these problems that are so common.

The principles in this training series are useful to everyone ... no matter where you are in the 20–60–20 ratio.

In a Living Free small group, a safe place is created where people can examine their lives honestly before God and can experience change and growth with the help of brothers and sisters. Getting free from our struggles doesn't happen by chance, and it doesn't happen overnight. In healthy small group environments, God works as His people love each other and hold each other accountable to the standard of His Word.

Take some time now to pray that God will show you how Living Free will meet your needs and fit into your church or organization's ministry. How does God want you to contribute to the process? For further reflection read the scriptures below and jot down your responses.

Psalm 119:11
What is the purpose of hiding God's Word in our hearts?

Deuteronomy 8:3
If "man does not live on bread alone," what does he need?

Matthew 22:29
What was the error pointed out by Jesus in this verse?

2 Timothy 3:16
According to this verse, what are the real and tangible benefits of reading and obeying the Word of God?

Additional Scripture references:

Isaiah 59:14; Psalm 19:8; Psalm 119:129-131; Romans 1:16-17; Colossians 3:16; Hebrews 4:12; James 1:22-25

Application

Talk About It

Discuss the following questions as a group.

1. Think about what you've just heard. What one key idea do you want to take home from this segment that can benefit you personally?

2. Look at 1 Timothy 5:24-25 on page 9 of your workbook. What are some examples of things that might be bothering someone under the surface where other people can't see them?

3. Look again at the diagram on page 9 of your workbook. According to the video, this ratio describes most congregations. How closely do you think the 20–60–20 ratio model matches your church? Does it surprise you to learn that so many people might be struggling?

Personal Reflection

1. During the next week, think about what segment of the 20–60–20 diagram **your friends** would put you in. Would they say you are part of the 20 percent who do most of the church work, the 60 percent who may hide their struggles, or the 20 percent who are openly struggling?

2. What segment of the 20–60–20 diagram would **you** place yourself in? When you look honestly at your heart, do you see an issue that has more control over your thoughts and actions than you would like?

If there is a difference between your answers to questions 1 and 2, why is that? Journal about it in the space below. End with a prayer for God to help you be honest with Him, yourself, and others.

Segment 2: Mastered and Trapped by Issues

Introduction

DVD (13 Minutes)

As you watch the video, look for answers to these questions:

What is the relationship between life-controlling problems and idols?

How can an occasional behavior become a life-controlling problem?

How does a person become deluded about their life-controlling problem?

[Handwritten notes:]
- Even church activity can become idols
- experimentation, it makes you feel good.
- Social use — you make rules for yourself that make think you are protecting yourself.
- You can't say no. Become controlled by it
- Denial — you don't see it affecting you but others do.

Self-Awareness

Life-controlling problems can become idols.

An idol is anything that we look to for solutions that only God can provide. When we look to anyone or anything other than Christ as our primary source of meaning, self-worth, comfort, or fulfillment, we are in danger of having an idol in our lives.

When we follow idols, a choice has been made to look to the substance, behavior, or relationship for help that only God can provide. Following an idol will prevent us from serving and loving God freely.

What the Bible Says

"Put to death, therefore, whatever belongs to your earthly nature: sexual immorality, impurity, lust, evil desires and greed, which is idolatry" (Colossians 3:5).

"So I looked, and in the entrance north of the gate of the altar I saw this idol of jealousy" (Ezekiel 8:5b).

See also: Psalm 16:4; 115:4-7; Isaiah 44:17-18; Zechariah 10:2.

There are three main categories of idols: substances, behaviors, and relationships.

The most obvious substances are alcohol, nicotine, and other drugs, but food is another example. Behaviors such as gambling, shopping, pornography, television viewing, and work can become idols. Relationship problems are often entangled with substance and behavior problems and can enslave us when we try to control others or live to please others.

Life-controlling problems usually trap a person slowly and progress through a predictable pattern.

The behavior or substance abuse gradually becomes a normal part of life even before a person is aware. However, there is a predictable chain of events leading to a life-controlling problem.

A person is usually lured into experimenting with a dangerous substance, behavior, or relationship because it is accompanied by a "high" or feeling of exhilaration.

We call this pattern ***The Trap*** because it often snares its victims before they realize what is happening. As Dr. Jimmy Ray Lee, founder of Living Free, states, "Addiction is death on the installment plan. No one ever plans to be trapped by a life-controlling problem, yet it happens all the time."

Life-controlling problems usually progress in four stages.

The first stage is experimentation.

We learn that the substance or behavior makes us feel good. We don't notice serious negative consequences. Return to normal feelings soon follows isolated indulgences.

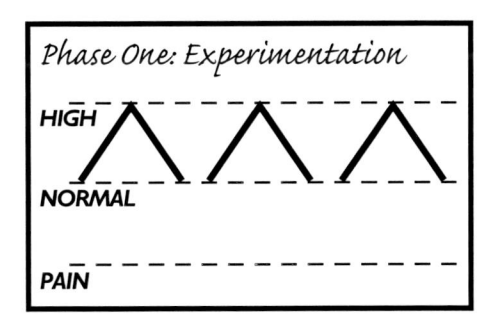

Phase One: Experimentation

HIGH
NORMAL
PAIN

Every person has the potential to experience a life-controlling problem—no one is automatically exempt.

In *Stages of Life-Controlling Problems*, Vernon E. Johnson, founder and president emeritus of the Johnson Institute in Minneapolis, observed (without trying to prove any theory) literally thousands of alcoholics, their families, and other people surrounding them. He writes,

> We came up with the discovery that alcoholics showed certain specific conditions with a remarkable consistency (8).

Dr. Johnson uses a feeling chart to illustrate how alcoholism follows an emotional pattern. He identifies four phases:
- learns mood swing
- seeks mood swing
- harmful dependency
- uses to feel normal

Many of the observations made by Dr. Johnson and others, including us, can also be related to other types of dependencies, although the terminology may differ.

The second stage is social use or practice.

In the social phase, we practice the behavior regularly but set limits for ourselves about when, where, or how we do it. The rules make us feel safe and appropriate. In reality, our trust is locked not on God, but on the behavior or substance. Normal feelings are punctuated with more frequent uses, and the individual seeks friends who also indulge.

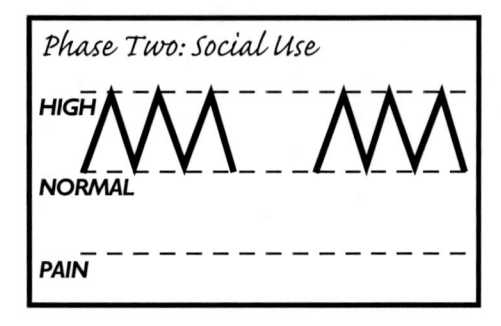

Phase Two: Social Use

The third stage is daily preoccupation.

Without warning, our behavior or the substance abuse becomes a problem. We violate our value system and begin to feel the pain of addiction. Life is deteriorating. We start to lose control and break our rules. The behavior or substance becomes the center of our lives.

By the time people arrive at stage three, their developing life-controlling issues are clearly idols to them. They are beginning to suffer negative consequences from their involvement, but instead of slowing down in response to the pain, they involve themselves even more deeply. They look to the behavior, substance, or relationship that is entrapping them for comfort and relief. Their delusion grows deeper until they no longer recognize the truth.

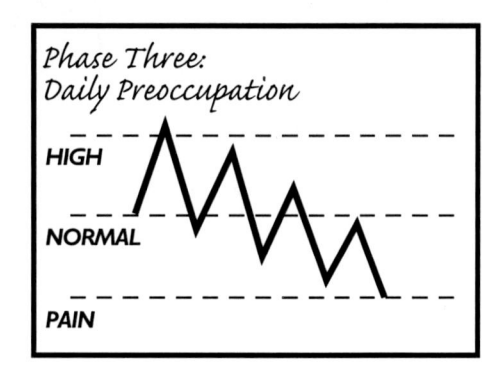

Phase Three: Daily Preoccupation

The fourth stage is using or practicing just to feel normal.

This is when we are using or practicing the behavior to feel normal. The only times we feel normal are when we are using the substance or engaging in the behavior. By this stage we're out of control. The pain is constant.

Not everyone progresses through all these stages; however, there is no way to predict which people who begin the pattern will continue to stage four. For examples of these stages in specific life-controlling problems, see the **Knowing More** section.

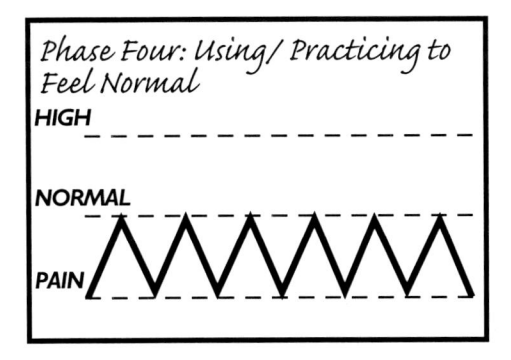

Phase Four: Using/Practicing to Feel Normal

HIGH
- - - - - - - - - - - - - - -

NORMAL
- - - - - - - - - - - - - - -

PAIN /\/\/\/\/\/\/\

Deluded people sincerely believe the lies they tell themselves and others.

When a life-controlling problem has trapped someone, they become deluded by the lies they tell to cover up their problem.

Denial is the refusal to believe the truth about our actions. People in denial know what they are doing is wrong, but they refuse to admit the truth and instead choose to rationalize their behavior. Continued denial leads to a state of delusion, a condition where people no longer recognize the truth about their actions; they sincerely believe their own excuses and become blind to the truth. Reality becomes distorted to them, and they live with a false belief system in which they reject the truth so long that they are no longer able to even see the destruction they are causing to themselves and those around them.

After a stronghold has developed, the delusion that blinds the person becomes very dark and difficult to penetrate. It is important to lovingly and patiently continue to confront the person's delusion and never give up—even when it seems the effort is not producing results.

Dr. Jimmy Ray Lee puts it succinctly: "Delusion is not seeing, recognizing, or acting in truth."

Jim Holwerda and David Egner, in their work on addiction, state:

> The fantasy world of an addict is more important to him than the real world. As he lets his thoughts go, he becomes convinced that the scenario he constructs to support his addiction is true. When shoplifters are caught, for example, they are often startled. The reality of the truth that they were stealing had been distorted. They had not realistically considered that they might face arrest or jail or embarrassment—the real consequences of their behavior.
>
> Along with distortion is a breakdown in logical thinking. The addicted person, for example, refuses to link alcohol abuse with impaired driving. Or sexual sin with a threat to his marriage. Or compulsive spending with bankruptcy (7).

Freedom from delusion comes when we gain perspective.

Because every person lives with a certain amount of delusion, we need honest relationships to see ourselves clearly.

The Johari Window illustration can help us understand how everyone is prone to delusion. Each pane shows something known or unknown about a person.

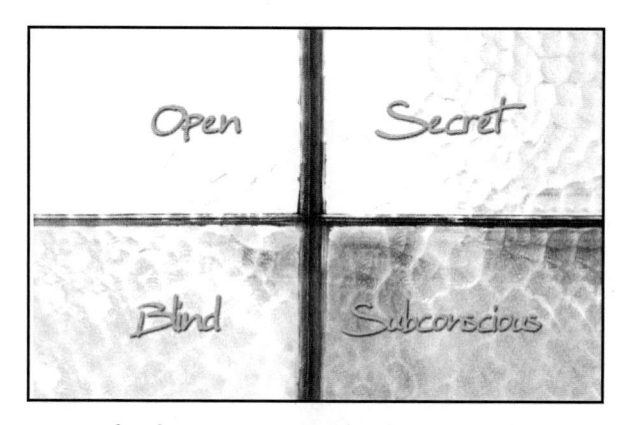

Joseph Luft, in Group Processes, describes the origin of the Johari Window. Dr. Harrington V. Ingham of the University of California at Los Angeles and Mr. Joseph Luft developed it during a summer laboratory in the 1950s. Johari is pronounced as a combination of the names Joe and Harry—the developers' names. (57).

The first pane is **Open**. This represents what we and others know about our lives. This includes the work we do, our hobbies, and so on.

The second pane is **Secret**. These are secrets known only to us and to God. As we begin to trust people, we may choose to gradually reveal some of these secrets.

The third pane is **Subconscious**. These are truths that neither we nor others see. Only God can see this part of our lives.

The fourth pane is **Blind**—the truths others see about us that we can't see. People in delusion live mostly within this pane. They need caring friends to give them feedback and to pray for them so that they can see themselves as they really are and recognize their need for change. The goal is for the open area of our lives to grow and for the blind part to shrink. We need the Holy Spirit to reveal the truth and give us grace to face the truth about ourselves that we have chosen not to see.

Spiritual Awareness Lead-In

Not everyone progresses through all the stages of life controlling problems as described earlier in this session. However, there is no way to predict which people who begin the pattern will continue to stage four. Proverbs 7:27 describes the path of a man on the highway to death who is tempted and succumbs.

Spiritual-Awareness

Let's look at some other scriptures that point to the progression of a life-controlling problem.

Luke 15:11-16
How does this verse describe the progression of a downward spiral in the prodigal son's life?

James 1:14-15
Describe the progression of sin and death in these verses.

Titus 3:3
This verse describes the road to enslavement. What leads to this state of a life-controlling problem?

Application

Prevention is the best cure

The best time to deal with a life-controlling problem is before it begins. Garth Lean, in his book *On the Tail of a Comet*, discusses Frank Buchman, the man whose ideas inspired change-oriented programs like Alcoholics Anonymous.

Buchman had learned that temptation, of whatever kind, was best resisted at its earliest stage. It was easier, he sometimes said, to divert a small stream than to dam a river. He defined the progression of temptation as "the look, the thought, the fascination, the fall" and said that the time to deal with it was at the thought. Tackle temptation well upstream (80). Myer Pearlman writes concerning this progression of sin, "A man is free to begin, but is not always free to quit" (54).

Everyone has the capacity to deny the truth to the point of delusion. Few people have the ability to see themselves as others see them and as they really are. That is why, in Living Free groups, we concentrate on helping people see themselves accurately by reducing the areas where they are blind to themselves. As we recognize and respond to the truth quickly, we are less likely to become deluded and develop life-controlling issues.

> "The weapons we fight with are not weapons of the world. On the contrary, they have divine power to demolish strongholds. We demolish arguments and every pretension that sets itself up against the knowledge of God, and we take captive every thought to make it obedient to Christ" (2 Corinthians 10:4-5).

> "They promise them freedom, while they themselves are slaves of depravity—for a man is a slave to whatever has mastered him" (2 Peter 2:19).

Talk About It

Discuss the following questions as a group. First look at 2 Corinthians 10:4-5 and 2 Peter 2:19, which are printed to the right.

1. Why do you think the words *stronghold* and *slavery* are appropriate to describe an area of sin that has become part of our lifestyle?

2. How do these strongholds limit our spiritual growth and ministry?

Look back at the stages of entrapment.

3. What reasons or excuses might a person give for entering the experimentation stage?

   The social stage?

4. What changes in a person might alert you that someone is entering Stages 3 and 4?

5. If a friend or family member were progressing through these stages, how would you feel about confronting that person with the truth? What would motivate you to choose to confront or not confront his or her delusion and blindness to the truth?

Personal Reflection

1. What excuses have you heard recently from someone you know who currently is living under a delusion?

   Have you ever made similar excuses?

   What behaviors or habits were you excusing?

2. Have you ever denied something that others believed was true about you? How did you come to know the truth?

3. Dr. Frank Buchman described the stages of temptation as "the look, the thought, the fascination, the fall." Look up either the story of David and Bathsheba (2 Samuel 11) or Achan (Joshua 7) and trace Buchman's progressive stages of sin in those accounts.

Handwritten notes:

- Delusion — Deluded people are actually sincere in what they believe.
- When we ignore our feelings we can become deluded about what is going on in my heart
- Bringing down the walls of defenses will free people from the spiral.
- face the reality of what they feel and do, is bringing the walls down.

Segment 3: Walls of Protection

Introduction

DVD (13 Minutes)

As you watch the video, look for answers to these questions:

What causes people to put up defenses?

What are some examples of behaviors people use to build walls of protection around their life-controlling problem?

How can Living Free help people let go of isolation, secrecy, and delusion?

Commonly Used Defenses

Acting superior	Intellectualizing
Agreeing	Joking
Analyzing	Judging
Attacking	Justifying
Blaming	Minimizing
Debating	Protecting
Defying	Questioning
Evading	Rationalizing
Explaining	Staring
Frowning	Staying silent
Generalizing	Theorizing
Glaring	Threatening
Grinning	Verbalizing

Self-Awareness

We use defenses to hide from painful feelings.

We want to avoid feeling the pain that being honest or leveling with God, ourselves, and others would bring, so we use defenses to hide from the truth. The defenses become walls that keep us isolated, deluded, and entangled in our sin. Larry Crabb elaborates on the concept of feelings:

> Christians often are confused about this whole subject of feelings. Some give the impression that if you walk with the Lord, confessing all known sin, then you will always feel good. Others teach that it is possible for a Christian to have negative emotions, but they must be kept under lock and key and never expressed. . . .

Bible Verses Concerning Defenses

Rationalizing
David rationalized Uriah's death: "David told the messengers, 'Say this to Joab: Don't let this upset you; the sword devours one as well as another'" (2 Samuel 11:25).

Blaming
"The man said, 'The woman you put here with me—she gave me some fruit from the tree, and I ate it . . .' The woman said, 'The serpent deceived me'" (Genesis 3:12-13).

Such teaching produces spiritual phonies. We all feel bad sometimes. And all "bad" feelings are not morally bad. Some negative feelings, even though excruciating, are perfectly acceptable and normal experiences in the Christian walk and can coexist with a deep sense of peace and joy. Other negative emotions result from sinful thinking and living. But even these should not be hushed up and buried, but should rather be dealt with by examining their causes and doing something constructive to remedy the problem (102-103).

God designed painful feelings to be a warning system. Painful feelings let us know when we need to pay attention to something in our lives. When we choose to ignore the negative feelings that result from our own misbehavior, we can become deluded about what is in our hearts. Buried feelings may explode to the surface when we least expect them, making our problems even worse. Two common feelings—fear and anger—are under the surface of many issues, although many other feelings can also be involved.

Defenses help us cover up sin and maintain our delusion.

Defenses can be used appropriately, but when we use them to avoid facing the truth about ourselves, they make delusion even darker. When we don't want to face the truth about our actions because of the painful feelings honesty would bring, we try using defenses to cover the truth or excuse ourselves. Each person has a favorite set of defenses. Some commonly used defenses are listed in the right column on page 23.

Behind most, if not all, defensive strategies lies fear of being exposed for who we really are.

When we use defenses to hide from the truth, we build a wall brick by brick. This wall protects us from the truth and provides a secret place for us to hide. Unfortunately, the wall isolates us from people who can help us.

Bible Verses Concerning Defenses Cont.

Denying
"Then the LORD said to Cain, 'Where is your brother Abel?' 'I don't know,' he replied" (Genesis 4:9).

Acting Superior
"For in his own eyes he flatters himself too much to detect or hate his sin" (Psalm 36:2).

There are three main tools of Satan that keep us trapped in our problems.

The devices that keep us trapped are delusion, secrecy, and isolation. Whenever we find ourselves or others being entangled by sin, we can see these three devices of Satan at work. To help one another live free in Christ, we need to be aware of how these devices work together.

Delusion is the first tool.

As we learned in Session 2, denial is the refusal to believe the truth about our actions. People in denial know what they are doing is wrong, but they refuse to admit the truth and instead choose to rationalize their behavior. Continued denial leads to a state of delusion, a condition where people no longer recognize the truth about their actions; they sincerely believe their own excuses and become blind to the truth. Reality becomes distorted to them, and they live with a false belief system in which they reject the truth so long that they are no longer able to even see the destruction they are causing to themselves and those around them.

After a stronghold has developed, the delusion that blinds the person becomes very dark and difficult to penetrate. It may take many attempts at lovingly and patiently confronting the person's delusion before you see results.

Secrecy is the second tool.

Secrecy allows us to hide. Even though delusion helps us justify our sin, we know that others would not approve of what we are doing, so some of us develop a secret life. This secret life hides our guilt and prevents those who care for us from helping. Life-controlling problems grow in the soil of secrecy.

Secret lives are deadly to the spiritual well-being of individuals and churches. Unless people have a safe place where they can deal with the sin that may entangle them, they will continue to be crippled by their secret guilt and shame. The ministry gifts that they could contribute to the cause of Christ will be lost, and the whole church will suffer.

Genesis 3 illustrates how Satan uses these devices of entrapment. The serpent lied to Eve, telling her that she could disobey God without suffering consequences. She believed the lie, became deluded, and sinned (3:1-6). Her husband also disobeyed God, and when they became aware of their sin, they tried to keep their actions secret and hidden from God. They became isolated from God (3:7-10) and from each other (3:16).

Delusion

Isaiah 44:17-20 speaks to the power of delusion in the life of people devoted to an idol. Isaiah comments on the blindness of a man who cuts down a tree and uses part of it to carve an idol, which he worships while the other part is burned to cook his dinner.

Isaiah says, "He prays to it and says, 'Save me; you are my god.' They know nothing, they understand nothing; their eyes are plastered over so they cannot see, and their minds closed so they cannot understand. . . . he cannot save himself, or say 'is not this thing in my right hand a lie?' " (Isaiah 44:17b-18, 20).

He says to himself, "Nothing will shake me; I'll always be happy and never have trouble" (Psalm 10: 6).

"The god of this age has blinded the minds of unbelievers, so that they cannot see the light of the gospel of the glory of Christ, who is the image of God" (2 Corinthians 4:4).

See also: Psalm 10:1; Jeremiah 23:26-29.

Secrecy

"Then the man and his wife heard the sound of the LORD God as he was walking in the garden in the cool of the day, and they hid from the LORD God among the trees of the garden. But the LORD God called to the man, 'Where are you?' He answered, 'I heard you in the garden, and I was afraid because I was naked; so I hid'" (Genesis 3:8-10).

See also: Isaiah 28:15; Colossians 3:3

Isolation is the third tool.

When a destructive stronghold develops in our lives, we isolate ourselves from people who love us enough to confront us with the truth about what we are doing. Concerning isolation, Bill Perkins writes:

> As the problem intensifies, their delusional system allows them to justify their isolation. Since they've learned to lie to themselves, lying to others is easy. Gradually they hold on to their idol with both hands, turning their back on the only One who offers them hope for deliverance (39).

Some of the people who drift away from our congregations may be isolating themselves because they are discouraged in their personal struggles.

Delusion creates a cycle of cover-up, relapse, and despair.

As long as we're deluded and hiding, no amount of willpower can free us from the issues that master us.

Hiding leads to a downward spiral of covering up our sin, repeating the sin, and feeling hopeless. We may resist for a while, but relapse is inevitable. We become ever more deluded, defensive, secretive, and isolated from natural feelings and from people who love us.

Spiritual Awareness Lead-In

God's Word is the foundation of instruction and direction for our life. "All Scripture is God-breathed and useful for teaching, rebuking, correcting, and training in righteousness, so that the man of God may be thoroughly equipped for every good work" (2 Timothy 3:16).

Isolation

"A man who isolates himself seeks his own desire; He rages against all wise judgment" (Proverbs 18:1, NKJV).

"The days will come upon you when your enemies will build an embankment against you and encircle you and hem you in on every side. They will dash you to the ground, you and the children within your walls" (Luke 19:43-44).

See also: Proverbs 21:29; Galatians 4:17; Ephesians 2:14-15; Hebrews 10:25

Cover-up:
Matthew 23:25-28; 1 Thessalonians 2:5

Relapse:
Proverbs 26:11; 2 Peter 2:22

Despair:
Psalm 31:10-11; Psalm 73:14; Proverbs 5:22-23; Proverbs 19:3

Living Free groups are focused on applying biblical truth to everyday life. The Word of God is the unchanging truth that confronts our delusion when we begin to excuse in ourselves the sin that so easily deceives and entangles us. God's wisdom takes precedence over any human opinion.

Spiritual-Awareness

God has provided us with three resources to confront delusion, secrecy, and isolation.

The Word of God Confronts Our Delusion.

God's Word communicates God's standard of righteousness, which is firm and unchanging. Society may redefine what is normal, permissible, and legal, but God's Word is the standard for what is right.

When we entertain delusion, believing that our sinful strongholds are acceptable, then, as Charles Stanley explains,

> Our responsibility is to tear down . . . strongholds through Spirit-filled prayers. How? There is only one weapon—the sword of the Spirit. We must fight these lies with God's Word. We must fight specific lies with specific truths (118).

"He would not taunt us with freedom and then make it unattainable. In fact, He will implement change in every heart made available to Him. Our job is to align ourselves with His spiritual laws, and as we do, transformation will occur" (Murphy, 76).

Hebrews 4:12
In light of this verse, why is the Word of God applicable for today's living and issues?

Psalm 119:89-90
Describe the faithfulness of God and why His Word is trustworthy.

"Your Word is a lamp to my feet and a light for my path" (Psalm 119:105).

The Spirit of God Confronts Our Secrecy.

The Holy Spirit confronts the secret areas of our lives with God's truth. Through the Holy Spirit, believers "put to death the misdeeds of the body" (Romans 8:13). Believers are "led by the Spirit of God" (Romans 8:14).

Whether the Holy Spirit leads by inward urgings or by circumstances, His direction is always in God's will, in agreement with Scripture, and in opposition to the sinful nature. We have the promise of the Holy Spirit to guide us through the maze of deception in this addictive society. Being our Counselor, the Holy Spirit will make Jesus known to us in a personal way.

The Holy Spirit guides us and empowers us, but He does not force us to change. We still have to choose daily to "put to death the misdeeds of the body" by the Spirit's power. Such choices sometimes take effort and don't always feel good immediately. The Holy Spirit makes freedom possible.

John 16:13
Where does the Spirit of truth guide us?

Acts 1:8
What does Jesus say about empowerment in this verse?

The People of God Confront Our Isolation

God confronts our tendency to stray from Him and to isolate ourselves with the help of the people of God. Hebrews 3:13 points to the importance of healthy relationships: "But encourage one another daily, as long as it is called Today, so that none of you may be hardened by sin's deceitfulness." The picture of this verse can be seen as a long-distance race in which the runner is weary and perhaps ready to give up. The encourager comes alongside to offer support, encouraging the runner not to give up. The encouragement is personal—for "one another"—and "daily." The word *Today* implies urgency; now is the time.

Why are relationships with other believers important? As Hebrews 3:13b states, "So that none of you may be hardened [a process] by sin's deceitfulness [the delusion of sin]." We need an active relationship with Jesus Christ and with one another in this addictive society. Building relationships with one another can be hard work, but it is essential whether it is in a Sunday school class, home group, office setting, cell group, or support group.

You need the people of God. The people of God need you.

Hebrews 10:24
What are we encouraged to "spur one another on" toward in this verse?

Galatians 6:1-2
In this verse, what are the responsibilities of a brother or sister toward someone caught in a sin?

Right thinking involves replacing the lies that we believe with truth.

When we are caught in a cycle of delusion or are unable to see our blind spots, we need others to gently confront us with the truth. Right thinking leads to right behavior, which in turn leads to right feelings.

> Counseling can be thought of as an effort to learn "right thinking," to choose "right behaviors," and then to experience "right feelings" (Crabb, 102).

Many of us spend years acquiring false patterns of thought and become unable to see where our thinking has gone wrong. A small group provides a safe place to look at these patterns confidentially with other people who care about us.

Help for an individual with a life-controlling problem begins with truthful thinking (thinking that yields to biblical principles). As people begin to change their behavior in obedience to God's Word, they will begin to experience right feelings. Although the development of a better understanding of oneself (self-awareness) is important, growth in Christ (spiritual awareness and application) should always remain the primary focus.

"Do not conform any longer to the pattern of this world, but be transformed by the renewing of your mind"(Romans 12:2).

Living Free groups provide a safe environment to grow and learn new patterns of life.

In Living Free groups, people have the opportunity to face the truth about what they feel and do. They can stop hiding and can open their lives to God. They can stop isolating themselves as they find people who love and care for them unconditionally. When the cycle of cover-up, relapse, and despair is broken, the result is spiritual freedom in Christ.

In an *Insight Group*, members learn how to help people with life-controlling problems, how to prevent those problems from developing in their own lives, and how to overcome existing life-controlling problems. Each person in the group has his or her own issues, whether he or she realizes it or not.

The typical *Insight Group* has nine sessions and expands on some of the basic principles touched on in the *Living Free* DVDs that comprise this series. After that, a person may choose to go on to groups that address specific issues or general discipleship topics.

Application

Talk About It

Discuss the following questions as a group.

1. Do you think being in a spiritually accountable relationship with others would help you in your spiritual growth? Why or why not? How could such an accountability relationship help you?

2. Describe the environment you were in when you last felt safe enough to talk about your personal issues. What qualities have to exist for an environment to feel "safe" to you?

3. How can we begin to "carry each other's burdens" and "encourage one another daily" as Galatians 6:2 and Hebrews 3:13 suggest?

Personal Reflection

1. Has there ever been a time when you tried to bury your feelings? What was the result of this action?

2. Are there painful issues in your life that you need to deal with in a different way than you have been? Read Psalm 32, which was written by King David after his sin with Bathsheba. What can you learn from his example about the right way to deal with your own struggles? What step can you take this week to break free from the issues that trap you and the delusions you hide behind?

3. Who (if anyone) in your life holds you accountable for your choices and actions?

Segment 4: *Family Influences*

Introduction

DVD (11 Minutes)

As you watch the video, look for answers to these questions:

How does one person's struggles affect those around him, especially his family?

What is meant by the term dysfunctional family?

How does a person's family of origin affect the way they deal with problems later in life?

Self-Awareness

Our struggles affect more than us alone.

One of the most damaging delusions we entertain is that our problems are not hurting anyone other than ourselves. On the contrary, one person's problems affect a network of personal relationships. The closer the relationship, the greater the impact. For example, our misbehavior may only slightly affect our job performance, but it may devastate our immediate family. This is known as the **domino effect**. If a husband is too involved at work, this may trigger conflict with his wife. The parents' preoccupation with their own issues, in turn, may cause one child to misbehave at school and another to turn to an eating disorder. As this happens again and again, relationships are destroyed.

We are part of a family system.

We use the term **family system** to describe the attitudes and patterns by which families operate. When one member of the family system has a problem, the others will deal with the problem according to the pattern they have learned. Each family member is an element in the whole, affecting and being affected by the system.

We can become more effective in helping ourselves and others when we understand that all of us are affected by a system of relationships that extends into past generations and that our actions will also impact future generations.

Some homes are more functional than others.

Even the most godly parents make mistakes. Many families are **dysfunctional**, which means there are relationship problems in the family that keep it from being an emotionally healthy environment. There are many characteristics of a dysfunctional family, and the following list includes a few.

- The children are the center of the family and are all that the parents have in common.
- When there is a problem, the parents blame each other.
- Family members are defensive and do not communicate.
- Problems and conflicts never resolve; they repeat in endless cycles.
- Parents are closer to the children than to each other.
- Authority is lax; children make decisions that parents should make.
- Authority is too strong; parents have no consideration for children's feelings.
- When a child has a problem, he or she cannot find help because one parent interferes.

When a family is struggling with the life-controlling issues of one or more members, the family can become too enmeshed or disengaged. Enmeshed families are so entwined that they have no personal identity; personal boundaries and responsibilities are eroded. Disengaged families have little or no emotional connection, so they must deal with their pain individually and cannot be supportive to one another.

James F. Crowley describes a dysfunctional system as "a family or group which communicates defensively within itself—reacting to one another in predictable ways." He goes on to say that "each member is locked into a survival role which perpetuates the system. One or more members must risk breaking out of his/her role and/or breaking the rules of the system for change to take place."

Ralph Turnbull says about generations:
Church and community are concerned with the stability of family life. Family instability contributes inordinately to human suffering "unto the third and fourth generation" (221).

Meir, Ratcliff, and Rowe state:
If we, as parents, live sinful and psychologically unhealthy lives, there will be a profound effect upon our children, grandchildren, and perhaps other descendants as well. God is not punishing our offspring for our sins, we are, by not living the right way (45).

In a **functional family**, there is a sense of family wholeness. Members have a feeling of belonging that contributes to their personal sense of well-being. Functional families have balance. People feel safe and cared for. Children are secure because they know their family loves them. Members are held responsible for their own actions, and when there is a problem, family members know how to help appropriately. No one person is the center of attention, and communication is open and honest.

In a functional family, parents do not place a higher priority on their children than on the marriage relationship. Parents exercise authority and strive to reflect the character of God's true nature. Functional families look different from each other, but they all share two characteristics: balance and age appropriateness.

There are no perfectly functional families, because there are no perfect people. All of us suffer some dysfunction, and that is why recognizing destructive patterns in relationships is important.

Children in troubled families learn three rules of behavior that they carry into adulthood.

Don't talk.

Children in dysfunctional families learn not to talk about the problems because if they do, family members will blame them for stirring up trouble. The dysfunctional family prefers to pretend things are better than they are, and they will punish anyone who confronts them with the truth. They are afraid the truth will only cause more problems.

Don't trust.

Children in these families learn not to trust because most of the promises made to them are broken. Dad may promise to take a child to a sporting event, but instead of keeping his promise, he becomes intoxicated.

Don't feel.

Children learn not to feel because they do not want to suffer any more pain.

It is important to note that functional families can have one or two parents. It is the relationships that count, not the way the family looks from the outside.

As Gary Smalley says:
Many child psychiatrists say children desperately need to see a genuine loving relationship between their parents. They have found that children who see a deep affection between their parents have fewer mental and emotional problems in life. Children whose parents are in conflict can lose their self-worth and can slip downhill into psychological problems (137-138).

Diana Baumrind (1967, 1978) identified three types of parents—authoritative, authoritarian, and permissive. She found that a combination of high levels of control and support, a style which she called "authoritative," is most conducive to developing competency in children. She suggested that an authoritarian style (low support and high control) produces children who have a respect for authority, but show little independence and only moderate social competence. Permissive parenting (high support and low control) tends to produce children who lack both social competence and interdependence (Balswick and Balswick, 95).

Children assume roles in families.

Children in troubled homes also develop roles they play in order to survive and cope with their pain. These roles are commonly labeled the Perfect Child, Rebellious Child, Withdrawn Child, and Mascot or Clown Child. While all children assume these roles to some extent, children from dysfunctional families play them to greater extremes.

Sharon Wegscheider, in her classic work *Children of Alcoholics Caught in a Family Trap*, describes those roles: family hero, scapegoat, lost child, and mascot. We have also observed these roles in other dysfunctional families where the problem was not alcoholism.

Hero

The **hero child** becomes a surrogate parent for the rest of the children by taking care of their needs. However, the hero child feels inadequate in the role of creating "normalcy" for the rest of the family. Although he or she may excel outside the home, inside he or she feels inadequate.

Scapegoat

The **scapegoat child** is, in a sense, the most healthy child in the family. He or she sees things the way they are and doesn't mind talking about these issues, even though this works against the "don't talk, don't trust, don't feel" rules.

As the scapegoat child attempts to talk about the feelings, everyone turns against him or her rather than focusing on the real issue. He or she is seen as the creator of the problem. This person, consequently, becomes angry and rebellious. He or she may turn to drugs or other socially unacceptable behavior.

Lost

The **lost child** is typically a loner. He or she is not a problem. No one pays much attention to this child. As a result, the child tends to daydream or fantasize. The lost child may seem independent but in reality is very dependent, lonely, and sad.

These childhood roles that often carry forward to adult life are described by Charles Leerhsen and Tessa Namuth.

A high achiever in school, the Hero always does what's right, often discounting himself by putting others first. The Lost Child, meanwhile, is withdrawn, a loner on his way to a jobless adulthood, and thus, in some ways, very different from the Scapegoat, who appears hostile and defiant but inside feels hurt and angry. . . . Last and least—in his own mind—is the Mascot, fragile and immature yet charming: the family clown (67).

Mascot

The **mascot** is the child who deals with all the family problems with humor. He or she relieves some of the pressure. Because of the mascot child, the family begins to feel that things are not as bad as they appear to be. This child may feel lost and inadequate or confused, yet no one knows this.

Various theories attempt to explain why some life-controlling problems seem to run in families. Some experts believe it is hereditary; others attribute it to a person's environment. Frank Minirth, a noted psychiatrist, has said:

> Alcoholism runs in families, but it is not clear whether this pattern relates more to hereditary or environmental influence. If an "addiction-prone" trait is passed genetically, the specific trait has not been identified. . . .
>
> There is reason to believe that there may be some genetic difference in many but not all alcoholics. But genetics is not the only reason individuals become alcoholics. Nor does every person with this genetic difference become an alcoholic (60-61).

Spiritual Awareness Lead-In

Our struggles may have roots in the way we learned to survive as children.

When we grow up in a dysfunctional family environment, we live with pain and chaos. We see destructive behaviors modeled before us, and we often carry these learned behaviors into our adult lives, recreating the type of environment we grew up in by repeating the mistakes of our elders. These behaviors handed down from generation to generation are what we call **hand-me-downs**.

Hand-me-downs are behavior patterns that have their roots in the family system and are helpful in understanding why we behave as we do. A child growing up accepts the behaviors they observe every day at home as normal because they have no other reference. As adults, people tend to create the same type of family relationships they knew as children. The influence of our childhood family is extremely powerful. Parents are leaving a legacy for their children that will affect them—either positively or negatively—throughout their lives.

> For I, the LORD your God, am a jealous God, punishing the children for the sin of the fathers to the third and fourth generation of those who hate me, but showing love to a thousand generations of those who love me and keep my commandments (Exodus 20:5).

Spiritual-Awareness

God's Word and influence can be handed down to the next generation. However, unhealthy paradigms can be handed down also. Peter described them as "the empty way of life handed down to you from your forefathers" (1 Peter 1:18). Futile behavior patterns, traditions, and lifestyles are often handed down from generation to generation.

There is hope for sons and daughters who have been handed down dysfunctional pain. Let's look at 1 Peter 1:17-23.

1 Peter 1:17
First, God is fair. Children reared by an abusive or neglectful father often have an incorrect view of God, picturing Him as their earthly father. The good news is that our Heavenly Father is perfect and fair.

Does the fact that God is perfect and fair remove our responsibility for our choices? Why or why not?

1 Peter 1:18-19
Second, Christ offers release from enslaving hand-me-downs. This comes "not with perishable things such as silver or gold . . . but with the precious blood of Christ, a lamb without blemish or defect" (1 Peter 1:18-19).

How does the precious blood of Christ bring freedom?

1 Peter 1:20
Third, Jesus knows each of us personally. God knew our need before the world was created, and made provision for us to be released from hand-me-downs.

What does this tell us about His personal concern?

1 Peter 1:22
Fourth, God will help you walk in His behavior patterns.

How do we cleanse ourselves and have love for others?

It is interesting to trace our family tree and even do generational behavior studies; however, freedom comes first by being "born again, not of perishable seed, but of imperishable, through the living and enduring word of God" (1 Peter 1:23). To live a life free from enslaving hand-me-downs, it is imperative to walk out God's behavior patterns.

> With God's help and an understanding of family influences, we do not have to repeat the mistakes of our parents and grandparents. Jesus can break the chain of dysfunction.

Application

Talk About It

Discuss the following questions as a group.

1. How would you define dysfunction? (Use your own words.)

2. What are some evidences of dysfunction in a family?

3. What is a hand-me-down? What is the purpose of identifying hand-me-downs we have carried from childhood into adulthood?

4. 1 Peter 1:18 says, "It was not with perishable things such as silver or gold that you were redeemed from the empty way of life [useless and foolish behaviors, learned behaviors, lifestyles, traditions] handed down to you from your forefathers, but with the precious blood of Christ."

   What emotional and behavioral hand-me-downs have you received from your family of origin?

5. If you have received Christ as your Savior, how should you deal with the "baggage" or useless and foolish behaviors in your life? See 1 Peter 1:22-23.

Personal Reflection

1. How would you describe the family system in which you grew up?

2. If you have children, what are you doing right now to ensure that their family legacy is a healthy one?

3. Take a moment to honestly examine your heart, as the host suggested on the video. In the space below, jot down some issues that you feel God is leading you to explore and change.

Segment 5: Helping or Harming?

Introduction

Handwritten note: Enabling is rescuing people from the consequences of their problem addiction

DVD (13 Minutes)

As you watch the video, look for answers to these questions:

How does a person enable a loved one's life-controlling problem?

What emotional stages do families go through as they come to terms with a family member's life-controlling problem?

What can we do to help people who are struggling with codependency and enabling?

Self-Awareness

We often do more harm than good in our attempts to help someone with a life-controlling issue.

When someone we love is in the grip of a harmful substance or behavior, we naturally want to help. But sometimes, in spite of our best intentions, our efforts are harmful rather than helpful, and we end up enabling that person to continue in the behavior. We believe we are being kind, but when we rescue someone from their responsibilities, we are actually harming them.

Melody Beattie writes, "As counselor Scott Egleston says, we rescue anytime we take responsibility for another human being—for that person's thoughts, feelings, decisions, behaviors, growth, well-being, problems, or destiny" (78).

To put it another way, "Enabling is any behavior which, however well intentioned, serves to protect dependents from the consequences of their use" [of a substance or practice of a behavior] (Krupnick & Krupnick, 22).

Enabling softens the natural negative consequences of a person's misbehavior.

Enabling allows people to continue in their self-destructive behaviors without feeling the painful consequences that might convince them to stop before the problem spirals out of control. Eventually, without enablers, people run out of options and hit bottom.

Enablers work hard to shield their loved ones from the consequences of self-destructive choices. As a result, the enabler brings pain upon themselves that really belongs to their loved one.

In their well-intentioned efforts to help, enablers may

- lie for their loved one
- allow abusive behaviors
- hide the truth from relatives and friends
- defend their loved one when others point out problems
- help them with legal difficulties
- change the home environment to accommodate the person with the problem
- refuse to discuss the problem with anyone

There is often a fine line between helping and harming someone.

Enabling is progressive. It begins by making small allowances for someone's irresponsible behavior and gradually progresses until our lives are dominated by trying to cure and control our loved one.

A line must be drawn to avoid the progression. **The first time you bail someone out, that's mercy. The second time, it is enabling.**

It's difficult to stop enabling a loved one, because we don't like to admit that we have no power to change another person. We must come to this realization, however, in order to help a person with a life-controlling problem. Otherwise enabling will progress to a condition known as codependency.

> We are all enablers to a certain extent. All of us need to look at whether we're helping or harming the struggling people in our lives. Although we can't change overnight, we can begin the process. We can start by telling our loved ones that we are going to stop harming them by trying to fix the problem or protecting them from their bad choices.

When we become obsessed with controlling someone else's behavior, we have a problem called codependency.

Codependency is a popular word used to describe a person's behavior when he or she is addicted to another person. Codependents take ownership of another person's problems, get their sense of well-being from managing the behavior of the dependent person, and end up being controlled by the person they are trying to help. They center their lives on the person they are trying to help, and as a result they exchange the truth of God for a lie, worshiping and serving a created person rather than God the Creator (see Romans 1:25).

Codependency is harmful because the person becomes mastered by a loved one's problem or becomes a loved one's master (playing God). As this person becomes an idol in our lives and consumes our energy, our relationship with this person changes. According to Kathy Capell-Sowder, there are certain characteristics that develop in codependent relationships (20-23).

> Melody Beattie defines a codependent person as "one who has let another person's behavior affect him or her, and who is obsessed with controlling that person's behavior"(31).

Symptoms of a codependent relationship

A person who has a love relationship with an addicted person will demonstrate certain symptoms:

- Increasing tolerance of unacceptable behavior

- Denial of the severity of personal impact and damage

- Compromising his or her own personal value system to manage pain

- Decline in major life areas such as spiritual and physical health, work, and family

- Feeling trapped in the role of victim

- Making plans to escape the relationship

- Developing addictions in other areas

Codependency and guilt feelings

Generally, people are not aware that they are enabling and becoming codependent. They are trying to do the right thing, but too often they feel guilty because their efforts are not good enough to make the person they love change. Children are especially vulnerable to this distorted, guilt-ridden thinking.

Codependent people often feel guilty because they believe that they did something to cause their loved one to go out of control. They see that their efforts have not cured the person, and they think that somehow if they try harder, they can control the person with the life-controlling problem. The misbelief that we can "fix" other people leads to a painful cycle of failure and loss of self-worth. Other people's behavior is something beyond our power and control.

"A hot-tempered man must pay the penalty; if you rescue him, you will have to do it again" (Proverbs 19:19).

The pain of codependency

Codependents and enablers live in a pain-filled world. They live in a world of shame and fear. The one they love cannot give them support, so they lose trust, shutting down their feelings. Because they are hiding the problem, they cannot talk to anyone. They suffer emotional stress that may result in health problems. To cope with this pain, they sometimes make poor decisions that lead to personal addictions of their own or other harmful behaviors such as extramarital affairs. They may lose faith in God.

Christians are vulnerable

Christians can be unusually susceptible to codependency. Sometimes when attempting to love others as Christ has commanded us, we slip into enabling behaviors that lead to codependent relationships. As Bill Perkins says, "I'm convinced that the church nurtures codependent relationships. At times we even inadvertently train people to be codependents" (76).

The subject of codependency should be approached with balance. According to the apostle Paul, the body of Christ should be interdependent (see Romans 12:7-16; 1 Corinthians 12:12-27). We need to avoid the extremes of selfish independence and codependence.

There is hope for codependents.

Codependents need encouragement to examine their own lives. This is why the *Concerned Persons* group is so important in the Living Free system. Because of their own delusion, codependents usually cannot see their own addiction to another person. It takes friends from the outside to point out this reality to them. They can find these friends in the group.

Friends of codependents can help by:

- Taking them to a *Concerned Persons* group
- Encouraging them to focus on Christ instead of on their loved one
- Modeling an honest relationship with respect and boundaries
- Care-fronting delusion
- Encouraging codependents to accept responsibility for their own actions

Codependents need to understand the "three Cs."

They did not CAUSE their loved one's problem.

Codependents should be helped to understand that their loved one is responsible for the choices that have led to addiction, no matter what the circumstances may be.

They cannot CONTROL their loved one's behaviors.

Trying to control the struggling person through manipulation, domination, and guilt only leads to a greater loss of energy. Codependents need help to understand that they cannot fix their loved one—only God can do that. Accepting this fact of powerlessness is the first step toward recovery for the codependent.

They cannot CURE their loved one.

Helpers should encourage codependents to cast anxiety on the Lord (see 1 Peter 5:7) and help them understand they are not responsible for their loved one's cure.

Becoming codependent occurs over time, and overcoming codependent thinking and behavior also takes time. We need to be patient, continually encouraging our codependent friends to build their lives and identities around a living relationship with Christ. As we model God's unconditional love while expecting people to be responsible for their own actions, people will learn to build healthy relationships with God, themselves, and others.

Families typically go through five emotional stages as they come to grips with a loved one's problems.

In her book *On Death and Dying*, Elisabeth Kubler-Ross describes a five-step process that dying people experience in accepting their death: denial, anger, bargaining, depression, and acceptance. According to mental health professionals, people experience these stages whenever there is any loss, major or minor. A family in which one member is affected by a life-controlling problem will experience much the same process. Family members may go through the stages as listed, or they may jump back and forth from one to another in no particular sequence.

It is important to understand these stages so we can respond appropriately to people at various stages in the healing process.

DENIAL

Families are usually slow to recognize the presence of a life-controlling problem in a loved one. The facts may be so frightening that they decide to pretend they are not true. To help people at this stage, we need to gain their confidence so that they can feel safe enough to admit what is happening to their loved one.

ANGER

When the family admits there is a problem, a common response is anger. Anger is a "safe" emotion for many of us, especially when we don't know what we can do to change things. We need to help people channel the energy generated by anger in positive directions and alert them to the danger of anger becoming a stronghold in their own lives (see Ephesians 4:26-27).

> Praise be to the God and Father of our Lord Jesus Christ, the Father of compassion and the God of all comfort, who comforts us in all our troubles, so that we can comfort those in any trouble with the comfort we ourselves have received from God (2 Corinthians 1:3-4).

BARGAINING

People want to believe they have the power to change situations. Many of us think that if we change our behavior, the person with the problem will change as a result.

We bargain, either out loud or in our hearts, with God or ourselves or the addict. We say, "If I do X, then will you stop drinking?" "If I do Y, then will you, God, push my loved one to deal with his anger problem?" "If I do Z, then surely she'll change." Bargaining never works, and the helper should encourage the bargainer to look closely at his or her powerlessness to change another person.

DEPRESSION

The most depressing circumstances we face are those we are powerless to change. A person in this stage needs hope and help in understanding his or her feelings. It helps family members to share their painful emotions, just as King David repeatedly shared his emotions in the book of Psalms.

ACCEPTANCE

Our goal is to help family members accept the reality of their situation. At the acceptance stage, a person feels free to turn a friend or loved one over to God. This is a time when the wounded emotionally detach themselves from the one they love so much. If the victim gets help, the people in the acceptance stage do not feel they have to receive the credit. They have accepted their powerlessness to change another person.

> Feelings of depression are normal. However, we should be aware that, as Archibald Hart states,
> When a normal depression doesn't remit within a reasonable period of time (at the longest two weeks) then it becomes a clinical depression and should be treated. . . . It is possible for a psychologically triggered depression to be just as painful and serious in its symptoms as any biologically based depression (48).

It is extremely important for a helping person to understand the grief process.

Without this understanding, a helper may give up when a person denies that he or she has a problem.

It may appear that the victim does not want your help or is just indifferent. If you as a helping person understand the grief process, you are not likely to take the victim's anger personally and bow out of the helping relationship.

Spiritual Awareness Lead-In

Only God can change a person.

The goal is to reach acceptance, putting the person in God's hands and allowing Him to work with loved ones on His time frame. We cannot manipulate or demand that a person change—only Jesus can change a heart.

As helpers, there are three things we can do to help struggling people:

1. Direct them to focus on Jesus.

2. Model honesty for them.

3. Hold them responsible for their own choices.

Spiritual-Awareness

The prodigal son's father was not an enabler—he allowed his son to be responsible for his own action—see Luke 15:11-32.

Luke 15:11-13
The son took his part of the estate and "set off for a distant country." What did he do with his wealth?

How have you experienced life as lived by either the prodigal or the prodigal's father?

Luke 15:14
How much of his money and material goods did he spend?

Luke 15:15-16
He was hired to feed the pigs. "He longed to fill his stomach with the pods that the pigs were eating."

He had hit the end of his journey. What in verse 16 indicates that no one enabled him?

Luke 15:17
What in this verse suggests that he broke out of delusion?

Luke 15:18
What in verse 18 shows he took responsibility for his actions?

Luke 15:19-20
He showed humility and took positive action. What was the action?

Luke 15:20-21
"But while he was still a long way off, his father saw him and was filled with compassion."

The son confessed his sin toward his father and heaven.

The father had faith that his son would return. The father showed compassion, but there is no record of him enabling his son. He allowed the son to be responsible for his actions.

God has established a principle of sowing and reaping, which states that there are consequences that result from our actions.

> Do not be deceived: God cannot be mocked. A man reaps what he sows. The one who sows to please his sinful nature, from that nature will reap destruction; the one who sows to please the Spirit, from the Spirit will reap eternal life (Galatians 6:7-8).

How can you see this spiritual principle to be an expression of God's love and mercy?

Application

Talk About It

Discuss the following questions as a group.

1. Do you think it is ever appropriate to shield someone from the consequences of his or her own sinful behaviors? Explain.

2. What would you like God to do in your life or in the life of someone you care about?

3. Families often go through five emotional stages when confronting a loved one with a life-controlling problem. Those stages are denial, anger, bargaining, depression, and acceptance.

    At which of these stages do you think people are most likely to exhibit enabling or codependent behavior? Explain your answer.

Personal Reflection

1. The host mentioned that we're all enablers to an extent. Do you believe that? Why or why not?

2. If you agree, in what ways do you think you enable others in their life-controlling issues? Jot these down below.

3. Take a moment to read again the parable of the prodigal son found in Luke 15:11-21.

    What motivated this man to return to his father?

    How does this story relate to enabling?

Segment 6: The Small Group Strategy

Introduction

DVD (13 Minutes)

As you watch the video, look for answers to these questions:

It does not take an expert to lead a group. What are the three things needed more than anything else?

What is the role of the facilitators in a Living Free small group?

What characteristics are important for a facilitator to demonstrate?

Self-Awareness

Small groups are the foundation of Living Free.

Everyone in Living Free, even a potential facilitator, starts with an *Insight Group*. This nine-week group expands on some of the basic principles we've touched on in the *Living Free* DVD training. After that, a person may choose to go on to groups that address specific issues or general discipleship topics.

In an *Insight Group*, members learn how to help people with life-controlling problems, how to prevent those problems from developing in their own lives, and how to overcome existing life-controlling problems. Each person in the group has his or her own issues, whether he or she realizes it or not.

This DVD segment portrayed an *Insight Group* to help you see the personalities, situations, and challenges you may encounter in your own group. Because the video illustrates coping with an unusual number of challenging personalities and situations, the group you saw is not typical.

For more information on *Insight Group* curriculum, go to www.livingfree.org.

Each small group has a facilitator and a co-facilitator.

The word **facilitator** means "one who makes something easier to do." In Living Free groups, the most important task of the facilitators is to create a safe place where it is easy for people to level with the group. Some people will fear sharing their struggles with the group. The facilitators help members feel safe in the group by . . .

- Keeping the group discussion confidential.
- Not pretending to "have it all together" or talking down to others.
- Being first to share until others feel confident enough to go first.
- Accepting people where they are without being judgmental.
- Never scolding or showing disrespect.
- Being gentle but persistent in care-fronting delusion.
- Being humble, knowing that any of us are capable of falling.
- Always being there before the members arrive.
- Creating an atmosphere of warmth and trust.
- Opening the group sessions with prayer.
- Promoting the ease of discussion.

In the first *Insight Group* session, the facilitator explains the group's purpose, clarifies ground rules, and monitors the group's comfort level. The facilitator urges the group members to speak within their own comfort levels and emphasizes that no one is forced to share. Confidentiality is stressed.

Facilitators must know their limitations.

Facilitators are laypersons, not professional clinicians. They need to know when to refer a person to a professional.

People using alcohol or other drugs, people with mental illnesses, those who are a danger to themselves or others, and those with other major issues in their lives may need to be referred to a pastor, a social worker, counselor, or other professional. We recommend that churches put together a list of resource people and agencies for referral.

Confidentiality is an ironclad rule in Living Free small groups.

Living Free is not a substitute for medical or psychological care. We never advise anyone to stop taking medication or cancel their doctor's care.

We give our time, compassion, and love solely as caring people who want to be channels of Christ's love to those who are hurting and desire wholeness in Christ. As non-credentialed persons, we promise no professional psychological expertise.

The facilitator's job is to guide the group toward the solutions that the Holy Spirit offers. He or she is not expected to have all of the answers—that is God's territory. If members have need of professional help, they should consult professional Christian caregivers. Facilitators and other group members are not qualified to offer psychological or medical care.

For more specifics on the role of the facilitator, see the **Knowing More** section in the Appendix.

A typical group format has four sections.

Introduction: This is a warm-up time when group members get to know one another. The group in the DVD modeled this section of the meeting.

Self-Awareness (20–25 minutes): This is a time when group members talk about the issues they're facing as they relate to the subject matter.

Spiritual Awareness (20–25 minutes): This is when the group discusses what the Bible has to say about these issues.

Application (20–25 minutes): This is a time to apply or brainstorm ways to apply spiritual truths to life issues.

This format is followed in all Living Free small group curricula and is explained in each of the facilitator's guides. Facilitators should always plan each session with this format in mind—each section is important.

In order to help people overcome their struggles, the group must be centered around Christ.

Small groups where Christ is the focus can bring wholeness in Christ to those who are struggling with life-controlling problems. Helping each other overcome life-controlling problems is good, but the emphasis should always be on spiritual growth. To accomplish this, it is important for groups to have a planned curriculum that focuses on biblical principles.

The wheel to the right represents a Christ-centered small group. The spokes represent the group members, and Christ is the hub. As the group members come near Christ, the hub, they also develop a closeness with one another.

When the group facilitators become the center of the small group—the spiritual or psychological gurus—group members may form a dependent relationship with them. Facilitators should stand hand-in-hand with group members, not as superiors.

If a philosophy becomes the center of the small group, an emptiness or even deception among group members is the likely result. Philosophies that mislead groups include intellectualism, speculations, or logical-sounding arguments that neglect Christ as preeminent.

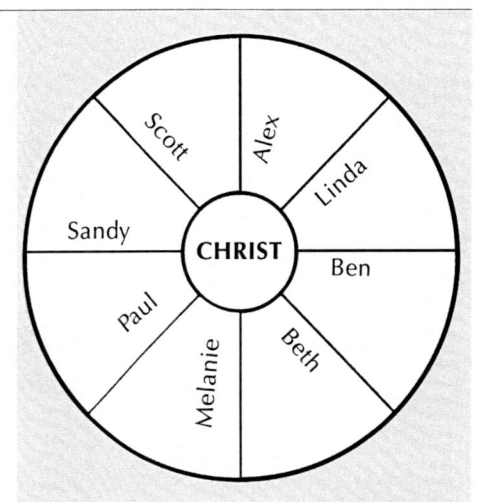

Spiritual Awareness Lead-In

So then, what is the facilitator's role in a Christ-centered small group? Through all discussions (pain, victories, misunderstandings, anger, opinions, frustrations, etc.), it is the responsibility of the facilitator to bring the discussion back to a personal level that focuses on Jesus Christ.

Spiritual Awareness

Living Free emphasizes Christ as the center of each small group. Paul writes, "For from him and through him and to him are all things. To him be glory forever! Amen (Romans 11:36).

Hebrews 12:2
Who is the focus in this verse?

John 15:5
Why is it so necessary to keep Jesus the center of our groups and life?

Colossians 1:15-20
Paul describes the supremacy of Christ in these verses.

> 15He is the image of the invisible God, the firstborn over all creation. 16For by him all things were created: things in heaven and on earth, visible and invisible, whether thrones or powers or rulers or authorities; all things were created by him and for him. 17He is before all things, and in him all things hold together. 18And he is the head of the body, the church; he is the beginning and the firstborn from among the dead, so that in everything he might have the supremacy. 19For God was pleased to have all his fullness dwell in him, 20and through him to reconcile to himself all things, whether things on earth or things in heaven, by making peace through his blood, shed on the cross.

Why are verses 17-18 so important to a Christ-centered small group?

Ephesians 2:22
How does Christ bring togetherness in a Christ-centered group regardless of social status, race, or gender?

2 Thessalonians 1:12
What is the prayer in this passage?

Application

Talk About It

Discuss the following questions as a group.

1. What proactive things can a facilitator or group leader do to make a group feel comfortable and safe?

2. If you have been in a group that didn't feel safe, what made that environment not work for you?

3. In what areas do you think you need to grow in order to be an effective facilitator? List these in the space below. (To spark your thinking, look at the qualities listed in **Knowing More**, pages 85-91.)

Personal Reflection

1. What benefits have you found in keeping Christ the center of your life?

2. What do you see as your role in an *Insight Group* setting?

3. Are there any issues in your life that you fear might be beyond your ability to handle by yourself? Are you ready to share these issues with others to get their help and support?

Segment 7: Effective Facilitation and Communication

Introduction

— Be there for them and don't judge them.

DVD (16 Minutes)

As you watch the video, look for answers to these questions:

What does a facilitator do? → pg 86

When we're talking about facilitating a Living Free small group, what is leveling?

What key things are important to remember as we're care-fronting?

Self-Awareness

A Christ-centered small group offers a setting where people can break free from their traps.

The facilitator and co-facilitator are crucial to the group's effectiveness. They start the discussion, keep it on track, and keep the group focused on application of biblical principles to personal life situations.

A facilitator needs certain qualities and skills to be effective.

IT IS THE FACILITATOR'S JOB TO . . .

- Open the meetings with prayer.

- Stick to the time schedule.

- Have a co-facilitator.

- Ask questions.

- Work within your limitations.

- Listen actively.

- Respect each group member's comfort level.

- Keep the group focused and on time.

- Share his or her own feelings and experiences at appropriate moments.

- Facilitate—keep the process going.

- Keep Christ at the center of the group.

- Set a tone that balances sensitivity and humor.

IT IS NOT THE FACILITATOR'S JOB TO . . .

- Do group therapy (open up deep wounds).

- Do most of the talking.

- Give advice.

- Judge.

- Answer most of the questions.

- Interpret what group members say; instead, reflect what they say.

- Dominate the group in any way.

- Forget to pray regularly for each group member.

A deluded person will tear down walls of defense by leveling with people a little at a time.

The video's group modeled the Self-Awareness portion of an *Insight Group* meeting.

They discussed a concept called **leveling**.

- Leveling about our feelings is openly admitting them.

- To level is to respond openly to God, ourselves, and others.

- We level when we take the risk of being known by spontaneously reporting our feelings. Our personal goal should be to replace isolation with sharing.

- In a safe environment, even a shy person will open up and level with others eventually. A foundation of trust is laid as the group bonds over several meetings. Some people aren't ready to share in the first few meetings. Others require even more time and patience. The important thing is that the facilitator doesn't pressure anyone into sharing beyond his or her level of comfort.

"But the tax collector stood at a distance. He would not even look up to heaven, but beat his breast and said, 'God, have mercy on me, a sinner.' I tell you that this man, rather than the other, went home justified before God. For everyone who exalts himself will be humbled, and he who humbles himself will be exalted" (Luke 18:13-14).

"He who conceals his sins does not prosper, but whoever confesses and renounces them finds mercy" (Proverbs 28:13).

Leveling isn't easy for anyone, but facilitators can help others be open by setting a personal example the group can follow and by modeling healthy communication skills.

You- and I-Messages

"You" messages

"You" messages communicate disrespect and judgment, thereby keeping people from leveling. "You" messages accuse the other person of doing things wrong. "You" messages tend to increase conflict by making the other person more defensive. They may cause the other person to feel put down, rejected, resistant, or unimportant.

"I" messages

On the other hand, "I" messages help open up pathways of nonthreatening communication. When I take responsibility for how I feel, then you don't feel so put down.

This type of message helps to communicate your feelings regarding the other person's behavior and its effect on you without strengthening the defenses of the other person.

"I" messages deal with facts rather than evaluation. They communicate honesty and openness. "I" messages are less likely to cause harm to the relationship than "you" messages. The self-esteem of the other person is not attacked. An "I" message is different from a "you" message in that the speaker takes responsibility for his or her own feelings.

How to Compose an "I" Message

YOU CAN FOLLOW THIS FORMULA WHEN LEARNING HOW TO FORM AN "I" MESSAGE:

"When" (describe the situation); "I feel" (describe your feeling about the situation); "because" (offer an explanation if you choose to).

Example:

"When you arrive home late and I don't know where you are or when to expect you, I feel afraid, worried, and eventually angry because I think you may have been in an accident." Contrast this to a "you" message, which might say: "You are so thoughtless, rude, and inconsiderate to come home late without notifying me. Can't you ever think of anyone besides yourself! Don't you care about my feelings?"

Examples of You-Messages

- You just don't care.
- You are a problem.
- Can't you . . . ?
- You are so . . .

Examples of I-messages

- I feel very angry because . . .
- I feel hurt when . .

Body language speaks louder than words. You can compose a perfect "I" message, but if you say it with threatening body language, it will be perceived as a "you" message. Be aware that your tone of voice, facial expression, and body posture communicate more powerfully than your words.

Care-fronting is confronting in a caring way.

Living Free groups employ a communication technique called care-fronting when it is necessary to confront delusion and denial.

We are most useful as care-fronters when we are not so much trying to change other people as we are trying to help them see themselves more accurately. Care-fronting works like showing people their reflections in a mirror or having them watch a video of themselves. They get a perspective on themselves that they cannot achieve any other way. This way the change will be sincere, not the result of manipulation.

Carefully frame your words to help a person level and respond honestly.

Carefronting risks conflict, but tries to minimize it by gently communicating in a way that does not make the hearer more defensive. We make it easier when we let the person know that we respect and care for him or her.

Focus your feedback on the action, not on the actor.

This gives the person the freedom to change his behavior without feeling personal rejection. Example: "When someone criticizes people who are not present, as you were doing a moment ago, I get uptight. I'd encourage you to say what you have to say to the person."

Focus your feedback on your observations, not your conclusions.

Comment not on what you think, imagine, or infer but on what you have actually seen or heard. Conclusions will evoke immediate defensiveness. Example: "You are not looking at me and not answering when I speak. Please give me your attention and answer."

"Then we will no longer be infants, tossed back and forth by the waves, and blown here and there by every wind of teaching and by the cunning and craftiness of men in their deceitful scheming. Instead, speaking the truth in love, we will in all things grow up into him who is the Head, that is, Christ" (Ephesians 4:14-15).

Focus your feedback on descriptions, not judgments.

Do not comment on another's behavior as nice or rude, right or wrong. Use a clear, accurate description in neutral language. When a value judgment is received, there is a momentary break in contact. Example: "I am aware that your reply to my request for information was silence. Please tell me what this means."

Focus feedback on ideas, information, and alternatives, not advice and answers.

Comment not with instructions on what to do with the data you have to offer but with the data, the facts, the additional options. The more options that are available, the less likely it is that a person will come to a premature solution. Example: "I have several other options that you may have thought about, but let me run them by you again."

Focus feedback not on why, but on what and how.

"Why" critiques values, motives, and intents. "Why" is judgmental; "what" and "how" relate to observable actions, behaviors, words, and tone of voice. Example: "Here is where we are; let's examine it."

Care-fronting should be done in a caring, gentle, constructive, and clear manner. Never care-front in a way that could be interpreted as blaming, shaming, or punishing.

Adapted from the book *Caring Enough to Confront* by David Augsburger. (Scottdale, PA: Herald Press. Used by permission.)

Spiritual Awareness Lead-In

It is important to provide an environment for healing and growth. Paul writes, "But we were gentle among you. . . . We loved you so much that we were delighted to share with you not only the gospel of God but our lives as well" (1 Thessalonians 2:7-8).

Spiritual Awareness

Eight Core Conditions of Helping

One way to create an environment of healing and growth is to practice the **Eight Core Conditions of Helping**.

Gary Sweeten, in *Apples of Gold I* and *Apples of Gold II* (adaptations of the work of Robert Carkhuff), shows eight qualities that are necessary for any person to be effective in helping relationships.

Thanks to
Dr. Gary Sweeten
Sweeten Life Ministries
P.O. Box 498455
Cincinnati, Ohio 45249
www.sweetenlife.com
and
Equipping Ministries International
110 Boggs Lane, Suite #301
Cincinnati, Ohio 45246
1.800.364.4769

1. ACCURATE EMPATHY

Philippians 2:3-4
How should we think of others?

Empathy is accurately perceiving what another person is saying and feeling. It is also communicating to the other person that you understand him or her while keeping an emotional separation. There is a difference between empathy and sympathy. Sympathy is feeling the feelings of another person and actually experiencing what that person is experiencing.

The following illustration communicates the difference between empathy and sympathy well: While walking down the street, a man heard someone yell for help. Looking up, he saw a woman standing on a fire escape, yelling that a fire had broken out in her apartment and asking for someone to call the fire department.

A. A sympathetic man would begin to cry out, tremble in fear, and identify with the woman. He would be immobilized by his emotional relationship because he could actually feel the same feelings as the victim.

B. An empathetic person would:

1. Accurately see the woman's need.

2. Understand her feelings of concern but not feel them to the same level.

3. Accurately hear her request.

4. Respond appropriately.

2. WARMTH

Romans 12:10
What kind of affection should we show?

Who should receive the credit?

Warmth is primarily communicated nonverbally through a smile, a twinkle in the eye, body language, and non-possessive touch. It is the opposite of being given the "cold shoulder." Various churches are often seen as "cold" or "warm" congregations, depending on the "climate" of the people.

By warmly attending another person, we communicate openness, love, and acceptance. This enables others to develop trust, and it lessens defensiveness. Warmth is a primary component in facilitating openness on the part of the seeker.

3. RESPECT

1 Peter 2:17
To whom should we show respect?

Respect is the most basic and most crucial of all the core conditions because it is most closely related to agape love. Respect indicates that I give people unconditional love, dropping conditions for acceptance. It does not mean that I cannot confront someone or hold a person accountable. On the contrary, it requires that I respect others enough to do just that.

RESPECT FOR ALL PERSONS WILL CAUSE US TO . . .

- Initially suspend all conclusions and judgments, looking beyond sin to the person.

- Avoid labeling people.

- Take other people seriously, treating them as equals, not as inferiors.

- Never offer quick solutions to problems but trust people to come to their own conclusions.

- Be interested in the person's concerns.

- Never show preference because of wealth, race, or social status.

4. GENUINENESS

Philippians 2:5-8
We find our best model for genuineness in the life of Christ. What kind of attitude did He show?

When we are **genuine**, we do not attempt to wear a mask on the outside to project an image of ourselves that is false. However, being genuine doesn't mean that you have to be brutally honest and transparent to everyone you meet about everything that is happening in your life. It does mean that you need to learn how to share with the world in an honest manner those thoughts, feelings, and concerns that are true to your own being.

5. SELF-DISCLOSURE

James 5:16
What are the two things that James tells us to do in this passage?

It is important to be able to share insights, experiences, and wisdom from your life as a helper in such a way that others may gain insight into dealing with their own issues and concerns. **Self-disclosure** is probably the most often used and abused of all the eight core conditions.

Self-disclosure is one thing that people do not need to be taught, because it comes naturally to us. However, because of that, self-disclosure is often poorly used as a sincere attempt to help others. We have to be careful that our self-disclosure does not become an inappropriate habit that closes off relationships instead of opening them up. Facilitators can develop a habit of talking too much about themselves; this will bore and offend group members. Effective helpers always listen more and self-disclose less.

6. CONCRETENESS

Luke 14:28-29
How does this verse deal with specifics?

Concreteness forms the bridge from the general to the specific. Since active listening opens people up to share large amounts of information in the process of self-exploration, it is important to consider how you might help people move from the general to the specific so that appropriate action can ultimately be taken.

There is biblical support for being specific in helping. One of these principles is this: Be sure to take all the facts into consideration prior to deciding a major course of action (this implies using concreteness). Biblical faith enables us to look squarely at the facts, yet have faith in God's deliverance, mercy, and power.

7. CONFRONTATION

John 8:11
How does Jesus use both caring and confronting in this verse?

Facilitators have to be able to **confront** people with the truth in a loving way to help them break free of their deluded thinking. Living Free uses the term care-fronting, coined by David Augsburger.

8. IMMEDIATE FEEDBACK

Proverbs 27:5-6
In what ways is immediate feedback which may include painful moments better for you than words from those who will not speak the truth to you?

When people in the group believe that you genuinely care for them, they will open up more. An important way caring is communicated is by giving people **immediate feedback** when they are sharing. Feedback is verbal and nonverbal, but it always communicates to the person speaking that you are interested in what he or she is saying.

Application

Talk About It

Discuss the following questions as a group.

1. In Colossians 4:6, the apostle Paul writes, "Let your conversation be always full of grace, seasoned with salt, so that you may know how to answer everyone." What do you think a conversation "full of grace, seasoned with salt" means?

2. In what ways are "I" messages helpful and "You" messages hurtful? Can you think of any times when you have used "I" messages to defuse a tense situation?

3. What is the difference between care-fronting and confronting someone? Which do you think people do more often, and why?

Personal Reflection

1. Can you think of a time when someone care-fronted you? Use the space below to describe how you felt during that experience. If you've care-fronted someone recently, how did that person respond?

2. Which of the eight core conditions of helping do you possess naturally? Which ones will be the most challenging for you to develop?

Segment 8: Launching a Living Free Ministry

Introduction

DVD (16 Minutes)

As you watch the final video in this series, look for answers to these questions:

Why is Living Free appropriate for everyone in your church, and how can it benefit them?

What are the steps to launching a Living Free ministry?

What are the ongoing needs and aspects of maintaining an effective Living Free ministry?

What does our congregation need to know about Living Free?

Key Points for Discussion and Reflection

Living Free can benefit everyone in the church, because we all have struggles and problems.

Every week, people of all ages go to church, their jobs and school giving the impression on the outside that all is well in their lives. But inside many are struggling or harboring secret pain. They may feel trapped by issues that are controlling their lives. It could be a relationship problem. Anger or bitterness. Pride. Abuse of alcohol, drugs, credit cards, or the internet. The list goes on because we live in an addictive culture that touches most of us.

Many of these people could benefit from individualized concern or counsel from a pastor, but pastors can't possible handle all of the problems and struggles in their church and community. That's where Living Free comes in.

Using biblically based principles, Living Free groups give people a safe place to deal with the private pain that rarely surfaces in public situations. It's also a place where you can learn to help others—family members and friends—to avoid life-controlling problems.

In today's churches and communities, we see the need more and more for relationship-based ministry so that we can help each other deal with struggles we face in daily living. Churches need a healthy combination of corporate worship of God and small groups that focus on relationships and felt needs, drawing people to turn to Jesus and the Word of God to find answers.

You might feel that you don't need this kind of ministry, but your presence may be the very difference in someone's life. God calls us to share our lives with others. If you are willing to share your life with others in this small group ministry, you may turn out to be a lifesaver to someone who desperately needs help ... and in the process, you just might find that you have had needs in your life met as well.

How do you get started? It's easy, if you follow the steps on the next page.

> "We loved you so much that we were delighted to share with you not only the gospel of God but our lives as well, because you had become so dear to us ... For you know that we dealt with each of you as a father deals with his own children, encouraging, comforting and urging you to live lives worthy of God, who calls you into his kingdom and glory" (1 Thessalonians 2:8,11-12 NIV).

Steps to Establishing an Effective Living Free Ministry.

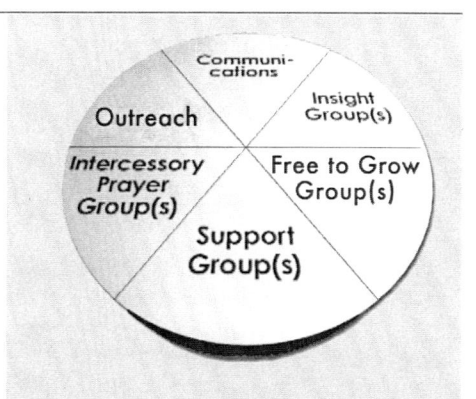

1. **Conduct the Living Free training.** This DVD training series can benefit anyone in the church, so the first step is to expose as many people as possible in your congregation to the DVD training described in this book. You do the training yourself or have one of our nationally-certified faculty come to your church and lead the session for you.

2. **Conduct initial *Insight Groups* for your facilitators and any other interested leaders.** Everyone who becomes a Living Free facilitator needs to go through an *Insight Group*. From the group you train using the Living Free curriculum, you should choose facilitators and co-facilitators to conduct your *Insight Groups*.

3. **Appoint a Living Free team leader (Coordinator) and form your Core Leadership Team.** After conducting the first *Insight Group*, you should have a good idea of who should be on your Core Team. Those people who have a heart and an aptitude for leading groups should be chosen by the church leadership to serve. The *Core Team Manual* that you can order from Living Free provides step-by-step guidance. This group, led by a Core Team Coordinator, will implement the Living Free ministry in your church and will help facilitate follow-up small groups.

4. **Identify the topics for the small groups you will offer.** The Core Team should plan the next groups to be offered after the *Insight Group* based upon the needs of your congregation and community. Living Free has a wide range of small group resources for support groups of all types. Normally a church will have an *Insight Group* forming at regular intervals as new people express an interested in joining. We suggest everyone participate in the *Insight Group* as a prerequisite for joining the other groups. You will also want to provide *Free to Grow* groups—these groups are specifically designed to minister to those who have experienced setbacks or disappointment. *Free to Grow* prepares participants for the "Appropriate Ministry" phase.

Insight Groups are for everyone, not just those with obvious struggles.

Most people shy away from categories or labels, particularly those they see as negative. The Core Team should be encouraged to focus the ministry toward the mainstream of the congregation, not just to the people with obvious problems. Labels (addict, dependent, sick) should be avoided. The **Insight Group** is a valuable tool of spiritual self-evaluation for any Christian.

Our Living Free curriculum is continually being updated, with new study options added regularly. Check our website periodically to see what studies might be most appropriate for the needs in your church or community.

5. **Establish an intercessory prayer group—** or incorporate prayer for Living Free into an existing prayer group. Prayer is essential to helping people overcome life-controlling problems.

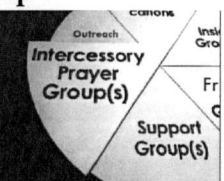

6. **Plan for outreach.** Many churches have found that segments 1-5 of the *Living Free* DVD training and the *Insight Group* are excellent entry points for outreach.

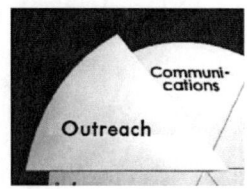

7. **Develop a communications plan.** Determine the most effective ways to get the word out about your new Living Free ministry. The Living Free promo DVD, testimonies, bulletins inserts, and flyers are all excellent ways to publicize.

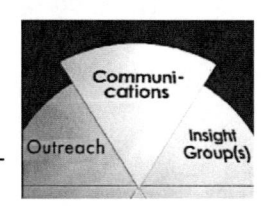

8. **Implement the Living Free flow chart described next.**

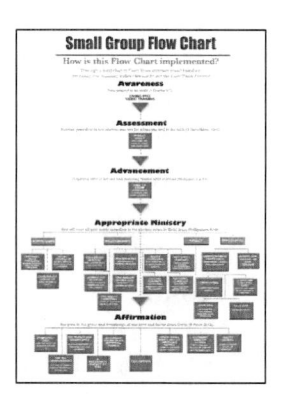

The Big Picture

The DVD training you have just covered in this guide is just the entry point to the Living Free group ministry. For your church to have a viable, ongoing Living Free ministry, it is best to follow the process described in the flow chart on the next page. The goal is to move down the flow chart from creating **Awareness** of life-controlling problems to **Affirmation** of people to "live free."

AWARENESS

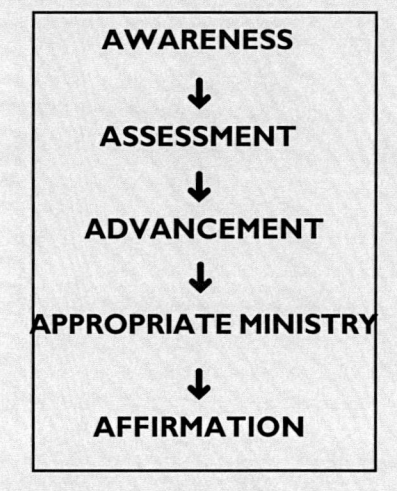

Living Free Small Group Flow Chart

The 8-segment *Living Free* DVD training that you have just completed increases people's awareness of life-controlling problems and their destructive impact on our spiritual lives and relationships. It also shows us how to help others through Christ-centered small groups. The first five segments of *Living Free* are ideal for the entire congregation and are used by many churches as an outreach ministry. This *Living Free* DVD series can also serve as an introduction to life-controlling problems while participants are waiting for an *Insight Group* to start.

ASSESSMENT

The Bible encourages us to examine from time to time where we are spiritually or have spiritual tune-ups. *Insight Groups*, which follow the *Living Free* DVD training, provide a setting for this self-assessment. Everyone who wishes to be a facilitator using Living Free small group materials should go through an *Insight Group*.

ADVANCEMENT

The third component of the overarching Living Free ministry process is called "Advancement." After going through an *Insight Group*, interested participants can use the *Free to Grow* curriculum that helps them explore disappointments and setbacks that may be keeping them "stuck" in their issues.

APPROPRIATE MINISTRY

Depending on the needs and interests within your community, your Core Team should prayerfully select the appropriate support groups to offer. New curriculum is developed regularly, but in general, the nearly two dozen small group options from Living Free focus on various aspects of addictions, relationships, mercy, and emotions.

AFFIRMATION

To fully live free in Christ, we need to grow in grace and knowledge. Living Free curriculum affirms our faith by offering a range of studies designed to help us with our spiritual walk in today's culture. Topics are listed on the next page and include studies on themes such as *Godly Heroes*, *Knowing God My Father*, *Completely Free*, and *The Ten Commandments*.

On the next page, you will see a similar flow chart that gives a sampling of Living Free small group materials that are designed for each phase of this process. Curriculum is being developed and updated regularly.

The small group materials from Living Free are designed to move people through this five-phase process to prevent and confront life-controlling problems:

AWARENESS
↓
ASSESSMENT
↓
ADVANCEMENT
↓
APPROPRIATE MINISTRY
↓
AFFIRMATION

Small Group Flow Chart

How is this Flow Chart implemented in Church-based Ministry?

Through a local church Core Team (ministry team) based on
the *Living Free* Training DVD (Session 8) and the *Living Free* Team Manual

Awareness
Train yourself to be godly (1 Timothy 4:7).

LIVING FREE VIDEO TRAINING

Assessment
Examine yourselves to see whether you are [or where you are] in the faith (2 Corinthians 13:5).

INSIGHT GROUP — DISCOVER THE PATH TO CHRISTIAN CHARACTER

Advancement
Forgetting what is behind and straining toward what is ahead (Philippians 3:13).

FREE TO GROW — OVERCOMING SETBACKS AND DISAPPOINTMENTS

Appropriate Ministry
God will meet all your needs according to his glorious riches in Christ Jesus (Philippians 4:19).

ADDICTIONS
- **STEPPING INTO FREEDOM** — A CHRIST-CENTERED TWELVE-STEP PROGRAM
- **SEEING YOURSELF IN GOD'S IMAGE** — OVERCOMING ANOREXIA AND BULIMIA
- **CROSSROADS** — CHOOSING THE ROAD TO SEXUAL PURITY

RELATIONSHIPS
- **CONCERNED PERSONS** — BECAUSE WE NEED EACH OTHER
- **PEACEMAKING** — RESPONDING TO CONFLICT BIBLICALLY
- **COMMITTED COUPLES** — GOD'S PLAN FOR MARRIAGE AND THE FAMILY
- **ONE NATION UNDER GOD** — TOWARD RACE RECONCILIATION
- **THE SINGLE CHRISTIAN** — LIVING AS ONE IN A WORLD OF TWOS
- **GODLY PARENTING** — PARENTING SKILLS AT EACH STAGE OF GROWTH
- **RESTORING FAMILIES** — OVERCOMING ABUSIVE RELATIONSHIPS THROUGH CHRIST
- **LESSONS LEARNED** — MOVING FROM HOMOSEXUALITY TO HOLINESS
- **GROWING THROUGH DIVORCE** — PRACTICAL GUIDANCE WHEN FACING DIVORCE

MERCY
- **UNDERSTANDING DEPRESSION** — OVERCOMING DESPAIR THROUGH CHRIST
- **CAREGIVING** — CARING FOR AGED PARENTS
- **SAVE ONE** — A GUIDE TO EMOTIONAL HEALING AFTER ABORTION

EMOTIONAL
- **ANGER: OUR MASTER OR OUR SERVANT**
- **HANDLING LOSS AND GRIEF** — HOW TO FACE LOSSES IN LIFE AND GRIEVE CHRISTIANLY
- **SAVE ONE** — THE MEN'S STUDY

Affirmation
But grow in the grace and knowledge of our Lord and Savior Jesus Christ (2 Peter 3:18).

- **COMPLETELY FREE** — A GROUP STUDY OF ROMANS 1-8 AND 12
- **THE TEN COMMANDMENTS** — APPLYING THE FOUNDATIONS OF LIVING TO MY PERSONAL LIFE
- **THE SEARCH FOR SIGNIFICANCE** — BUILDING SELF-WORTH THROUGH THE LOVE OF CHRIST
- **AUTHENTIC LIVING IN AN ARTIFICIAL WORLD**
- **A PASSIONATE PURSUIT OF GOD**
- **CELL GROUPS**
- **DISCOVERING GOD'S WAY OF HANDLING MONEY** — LEARN TO MANAGE MONEY CORRECTLY
- **KNOWING GOD MY FATHER** — APPLYING THE NAMES OF GOD TO MY PERSONAL LIFE
- **GODLY HEROES** — A SMALL GROUP STUDY OF HEBREWS 11

Participant's Guide: Living Free DVD Training, Living Free®, P. O. Box 22127, Chattanooga, TN 37422-2127

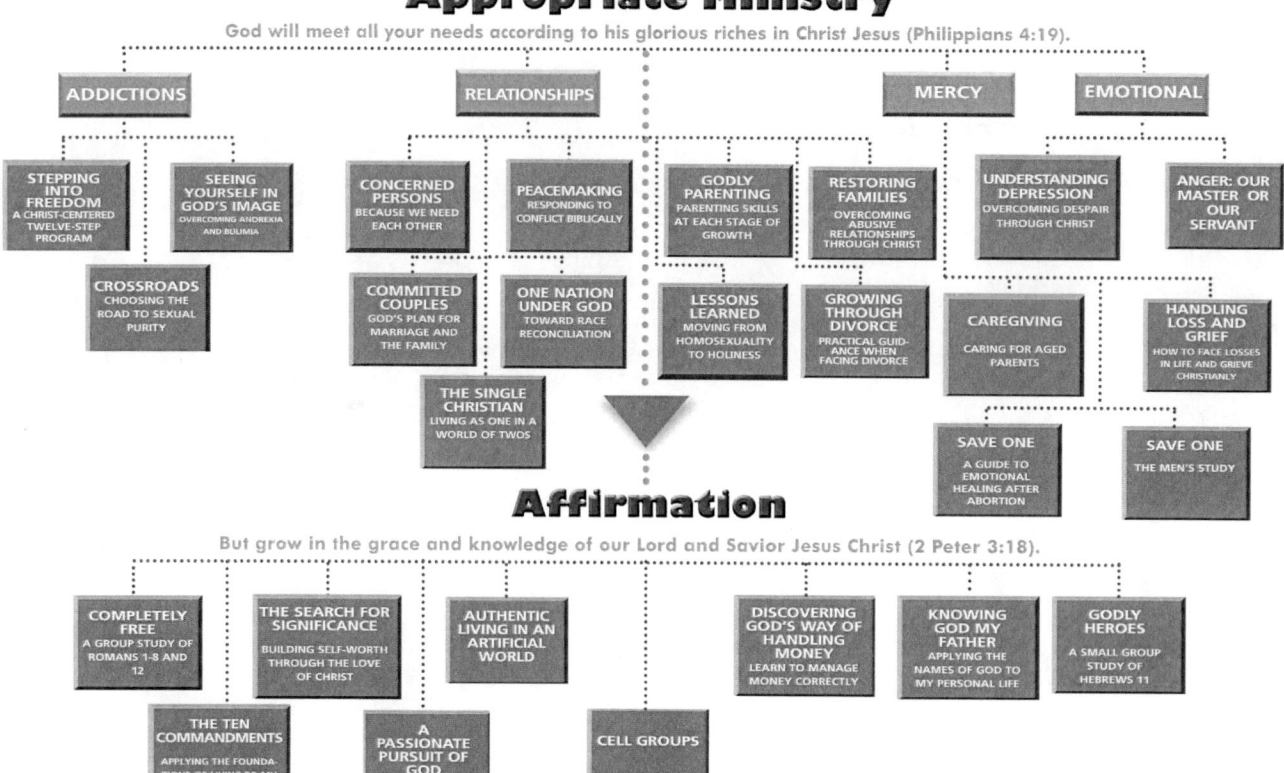

Launching a Living Free™ Community-based Ministry

Objectives

Referral The Living Free Community (LFC) ministry gives referrals to the counseling ministry and to long term residential programs like Teen Challenge.

Relationship LFC provides support groups for discipleship and accountability while developing a sense of community.

Re-Alignment LFC works to restore family relationships. Often participants marry their long time boyfriend or girlfriend who also may be the mother or father of their children.

Re-Establishment The LFC ministries also provide a great follow up for residential program graduates so they will have a place for accountability, building community and service

1. Pastor selects people to form a **Living Free Community Ministry Team** or Living Free™ will come and train the entire congregation.
2. When the LFC ministry team is formed and a leader is chosen (6-12 people taking on specific responsibilities; see manual for role descriptions), the next step is to make sure each team member goes through the Living Free™ DVD Training (8 - 45 minute sessions), LF can provide the training.
3. LFC Team members participant in an ***Insight Group*** with each person taking turns facilitating each session.
4. While the LFC team is going through the ***Insight Group***, the Team Leader(s) meet with the local jail chaplain and administrators to present a plan and request times for Living Free™ Groups in the jail. A minimum of 1-2 times per week is suggested, or the Living Free Team plans for groups in their church or neutral location.
5. After the jail agrees on a time, all volunteers usually have to go through training that the jail requires for anyone going on the inside.
6. An orientation group is created and meets in the jail one time per week (once for men and once for women depending on if you have women helping with the ministry). This group acts as a filter to see which inmates are serious about getting help. For example, use the first 5 sessions in the ***Living Free Participant's Guide*** for this orientation. There are 5 sessions and people could be required to attend to 4 out of 5 sessions to qualify for the program.
7. For participants who complete orientation, start ***Insight Groups*** using the Group Member's Guide once a week for 9 sessions and require participants to attend 8 out of 9. It is important to keep good attendance records.
8. Start Anger Management Groups using the LF Anger curriculum for 9 sessions.
9. When the participant approaches completion of the orientation, ***Insight*** and 3 weeks of the anger management group, present each participant to the prosecutor, parole officer and any others with paperwork determining that the participant is recommended for release. The courts generally will not sentence participants, but if a Living Free™ Representative (Court Liaison) is present during court they can recommend to the judge that the participant be given the option to continue their recovery on the outside by attending Monday night support groups and Thursday evening Community and by calling their coach the other 5 nights of the week.

   NOTE: It is recommended that there be random drug testing for participants.
10. After you have people starting to get released, have the participant call the LFC Team Leader for further instructions. The LFC Team Leader will assign the participant to a location (In the beginning, the participants could either attend groups at your church or a neutral location and then as the ministry expands to satellite campuses, the participant could be referred to a group close to their home). We recommend that you not get into providing housing. There are other ministries who provide housing so we suggest partnering with those ministries who can provide housing, transportation to the group meetings and job skills training.

Launching a Living Free™ Community Ministry

Structure of the Ministry: One Year Non-Residential
At the Local Church or Neutral Site ("On the Outside")

Monday Night Support Groups

(Not in sequential order therefore anyone can come into these groups at any time). We do recommend having one open group for walk-ons and for those who need a group but there are none available at the time. We suggest that all of the other groups close after the 3rd session (This allows trust to be built among group members)

Monday Night (or another night • 6:00 pm-7:30 pm each week)

- **INITIAL GROUP:** *Stepping into Freedom* – 12 step study (12 weeks)
- **SECOND GROUP:** *Insight Group – Character Development Study* (9 weeks)
- **THIRD GROUP:** *Peacemaking – Conflict Resolution* (12 weeks)
- **FOURTH GROUP:** *Free to Grow – Overcoming Disappointments* (12 weeks)
- **FIFTH GROUP:** *Concerned Persons – Overcoming Codependency* (9 weeks)
- **SIXTH GROUP:** *Anger Management – Anger: Our Master or Our Servant* (9 weeks)
  -or- topic based on presenting needs such as sexual addiction issues, depression and other topics.

Random Drug Testing for Participants
(Usually done by a volunteer medical professional a couple of times per month)

Thursday Night Community

Thursday Night *(or another night • 6 pm-7:30 pm each week)*

- Free meal provided to participants and their families
- Praise and Worship if available
- Opportunity to share testimonies
- A Short devotional from a pastor or LFC team leader
- Prayer

The Thursday evenings are a critical time to get the families of the participants involved in the recovery process. You can also invite pastors from other churches to provide meals on Thursday evenings and to speak for the devotionals. This is a great way to establish other LFC satellite campuses.

Sunday, Tuesday, Wednesday, Friday & Saturday

- Each participant is required to call their Life Coach to have a short conversation and prayer.
- Life Coach Training is available

Family Ministry

After the ministry is in full swing, you can create a family track on Monday evenings so that they can learn about co-dependency and enabling, overcoming abusive relationships and handling the loss of family through incarceration or death.

There is also the possibility of forming a support group for the children of the participants (*Empowering Kids God's Way - Insight for Children*)

This is one model of Living Free Community ministry. You can set the program up for people who voluntarily come to the meetings, but there tends to be much inconsistency.

People can come voluntarily from the congregation and community to the Monday and Thursday evening sessions to receive help as well. Some assimilation takes place back into the church when the congregational members become friends with the ex-inmates and their families.

More about the Coordinator and Core Team

Throughout this training, we have mentioned the Coordinator and Core Team for your Living Free ministry. As you can see, they handle many important responsibilities.

The pastor can suggest a possible Coordinator and can invite people to be on the Core Team. Or, someone in the congregation can volunteer to coordinate Living Free. The Coordinator schedules the Core Team meetings and is the contact for the pastor. The Coordinator also helps train new leaders.

Before Core Team members begin running the ministry, they need to go through *Living Free* training and participate in an *Insight Group* together. **This sends three important messages to the congregation:**

- Helpers need to know their own spiritual and emotional needs.

- This ministry is for everyone, not just for "problem people."

- Helpers need on-the-job training.

Living Free is not a one-time experience or a disjointed array of small groups. It is a process.

The foundation of any process-oriented ministry is a master plan. The Core Team needs a prayerful assessment of where it wants the ministry to go. This Core Team sets up a master plan and communicates it to the congregation. The *Core Team Manual* outlines the basics of this plan, which is comprehensive, detailed, and flexible.

In order for the process to keep going, new facilitators need to be encouraged and trained on an ongoing basis. Some churches may want to run the *Living Free* training using this DVD series every quarter or every six months. Every participant in the *Living Free* training should be viewed as a potential facilitator of future groups.

As noted earlier, facilitators need to be clear on the limits of their ministry.

Living Free small groups focus on spiritual, not psychological care. By following the curriculum carefully, facilitators can avoid making misleading claims. With that in mind, each participant should receive a written statement like the one in the **Knowing More** section in the back of your book.

Where to Go From Here

You now know all the steps to launch a Living Free ministry in your church or ministry setting. In summary,

1. Review and implement the 8 Church-based steps (p76) or Community-based Steps (p77) outlined earlier in this section describing how to establish an effective Living Free ministry. You have already completed the first step—you conducted the *Living Free* training using this DVD series.

2. Order the *Core Team Manual* and materials for the *Insight Group*, which comes next. Simply call us at 1.800.879.4770 or order from our website at www.livingfree.org.

3. Repeat the process on an ongoing basis because offering the introductory *Living Free* DVD series (particularly Segments 1 to 5) are a good entry point for small groups.

Application

Talk About It

To close out this series, discuss the following questions as a group.

1. Why is a master plan important to the success of any ministry, particularly Living Free?

2. Satan is eager to stop our efforts to help people find freedom in Christ. What are some obstacles that could keep this ministry from getting off the ground? How can we begin to deal with those issues?

3. Look at the list of reasons why new ministries fail in the **Knowing More** section. How can we address these issues before we initiate Living Free in our church?

The Bible promises freedom: *"If the Son sets you free, you will be free indeed" (John 8:36).*

We pray that through your ministry, you will help many people walk confidently in Christ, free from life-controlling problems. May God bless you.

Knowing More

In this section are additional resources that will be valuable in helping you implement a Living Free Ministry, improve facilitation skills, and better understand the trap of life-controlling problems.

Considerations for Growing a Living Free Ministry in Your Church

- To be successful, the ministry will need the same priority given to other important ministries of the church.
- Everyone needs to understand that becoming a facilitator is a process of mutual discernment that includes the individual's desire to lead a group and the Core Team's agreement that he or she is ready to lead.
- Always recruit church leaders to participate in the groups. The more leaders that go through the groups, the fewer people will believe that the groups are only for those who are "really having problems."
- Avoid stigmatizing the Living Free ministry! People will resist attending groups where they are labeled. This is why you must promote the *Insight Group* as a positive experience appropriate for everyone.
- Teamwork is important—there is strength in numbers. Without the team approach, helpers are likely to become overburdened.
- Members of the Core Team should be respected by the congregation, trustworthy, and committed to Christ.
- The Living Free model is designed to be flexible. You can choose how to use it to best fit the structure of your ministry.
- After your group facilitators gain experience, you will want to reach out to your community to meet people where they are hurting.
- It may take some time to start a helping ministry for people with life-controlling problems. Some people will take the "wait and see" approach. They need support, but it may take time to gain their confidence.
- Facilitators should never make claims concerning a leader's ability or the group's ability to solve a participant's problem. Keep the focus on Christ and biblical principles.
- Confidentiality should be explained during the orientation session of the group. What is discussed in the group should not be mentioned outside the group. Facilitators should explain that confidentiality will be broken if people are a danger to themselves or to others (i.e., the revealing of suicidal tendencies or the reporting of child abuse).
- Group leaders should be aware of their limitations. Some participants may need the care of professional Christian counselors. See *Core Team Manual* for additional information.

Frequently Asked Questions about Living Free Groups

Q Can participants be added to the groups after they have started?

A It is best not to receive new members after the first or second session. Since each session builds on the previous session, adding new members after you are more than two sessions into the series will hinder the trust level.

Q Where do people go if groups have already started and they need help?

A The first 5 segments of *Living Free* are an effective introduction to life-controlling problems or you may want to have a topical subject group for people to join until the next *Insight Group* opens up. It is good to have *Insight Groups* starting every two to three weeks so new participants can join without much delay.

Q Do you suggest same-gender groups?

A It is okay, but probably not best for normal routine. Having same-gender groups could leave the impression that heavy and deep, secret problems are being shared and this may frighten some people from joining the groups. Since we live in a society of males and females, coed groups would deal with that reality. However, it is best to have same-gender groups if the emphasis is sexual in nature (abuse, addiction, etc.).

Q Should specific sexual sins or acts be discussed in the small group setting?

A No. The discussion of sexual sins often leads to lustful thinking among group members and may lead some to unholy bonding. For this reason a person dealing with a sexual sin should say that he or she is dealing with impurity and not discuss the details. For those who need more intense help that may involve details, we suggest that those discussions be with a mature, godly person who can handle the information.

Q Can the Living Free concept be integrated into a church that already has active small groups or cell groups?

A Yes. We recommend that all small group leaders go through the *Living Free* DVD series, which will help prepare them for meaningful ministry in this culture. All cell group participants will benefit from participating in the *Insight* and *Free to Grow* Groups and focused "Appropriate Ministry" groups as needed.

Frequently Asked Questions about Living Free Groups cont.

Q **When is it best to conduct the Living Free groups?**

A There are various approaches that churches use. Most churches take childcare into consideration. It is good to meet when childcare is available, or group members may want to hire a childcare supervisor with a collection each week. Some churches meet during Sunday School; however, the time limitations may hinder the group (i.e., you may want to start the group 15 minutes early).

Q **Should the same group leaders stay with the same group for more than one group series (*Insight Group, Concerned Persons, Stepping into Freedom*, etc.)?**

A Caution should be exercised about group members' becoming overly attached to group leaders or the group becoming introverted. It is probably best not to keep the same leaders and participants together for more than two courses unless personnel constraints prevent such planning.

Common Reasons Why New Ministries in the Church Fail

As you consider launching a Living Free ministry, keep in mind these four common reasons why new ministries in churches often fail.

Ministries fail if they don't meet a real need. Do you know the needs of the people in your congregation? Where are they hurting? What issues are causing them to struggle? Does Living Free address some of these issues?

Ministries fail if the minister does not give full support to the ministry. It is important that the minister publicly endorse the ministry, be involved in the launch of it, and attend initial meetings. When the minister offers vision and encouragement by treating the ministry as a vital contribution to the church's mission, Living Free small groups will be effective.

Ministries fail if they are poorly organized. Living Free has a definite organizational structure. Follow the structure laid out in our curricula to avoid this pitfall.

Ministries fail if they lack committed leadership. Core Team members need to have a clear responsibility and be committed to the ministry. Facilitators are encouraged to attend Core Team meetings once or twice a month. These meetings provide a place for facilitators to receive support and be ministered to as well as participate in planning.

Group Member Sample Letter

Below is a sample letter that can be used as a guide for participants. This letter gives important information about how your ministry is not a substitute for medical or psychological care.

Dear Friend,

Welcome to the (insert your ministry name) ministry of the _____ Church.

We are pleased you have chosen to be a part of this ministry.

Each person in our ministry is trained to listen, pray, and help others find biblical wisdom with which to guide their lives. Although we believe that all of us are created in God's image and consist of a body, soul, and spirit, our approach is primarily spiritual and biblical rather than simply psychological or physiological. However, we all attempt to live our lives and carry out our ministry in consistency with sound psychological principles that are in harmony with biblical principles. Each of our group leaders has been through a training program that emphasizes the importance of human relationships built on Christian theology and the power of the Holy Spirit.

It is important for you as a group participant to realize that we in the (insert your ministry name) ministry of _____ Church are not a substitute for medical or psychological care. We never advise anyone to stop taking medication or cancel their doctor's care.

We give our time, compassion, and love solely as caring lay persons who want to be channels of Christ's love to people who are hurting and who desire wholeness in Christ.

As noncredentialed persons, we promise no professional psychological expertise. However, we do have a desire to see the Lord help you with your struggles. We will join you in prayer.

Below are some guidelines that may be helpful to you as a group member.

- The _____ group will meet on _____ evenings.
- Sessions will start at _____ and conclude by _____.
- Our groups are normally led by two group facilitators.
- Please call in advance if you cannot attend a group meeting.

(Your name)

(Your ministry name)

Coordinator, _____ Church

Important Qualities of Effective Group Leaders

CHRISTLIKENESS
As leaders we no longer can be "lost in the crowd," just doing our own thing, unconcerned about what others think. Those we lead may imitate our example—the places we go, the things we do, and what we say. If our actions are not Christlike, we will lead them down the wrong path. Ask yourself this question: "Is Jesus pleased with what I am doing and saying?" Remember, you are an example that others will follow.

THE SPIRIT OF A SERVANT
God places us in ministry so that we might serve, love, and care for those we lead. We must never feel we can rule or dictate to others. Keep in mind that even God respects a person's free will. Leadership is for the purpose of serving.

A SHEPHERD'S HEART
It is important to see beyond present difficulties and to recognize the amazing potential for change that each group member has in Christ. A shepherd will exhibit firm love and gentle encouragement in the process of leading people to a richer relationship with God. We accept people as they are, so we help them become all God intends them to be.

LOVE AND HOSPITALITY
This involves giving of yourself—even to those who are unlovely. The Amplified Bible speaks boldly of this subject in 1 Peter 4:9: "Practice hospitality to one another—that is, those of the household of the faith."

ANOINTED ENTHUSIASM
Your small group will never exceed your personal plateau of enthusiasm. If you don't get inspired and motivated about what you are leading and doing, neither will anyone else! Usually people are not projecting as much enthusiasm as they think they are.

A TEACHABLE SPIRIT
Every facilitator has room for improvement, and the ability to accept constructive criticism without being defensive is a great strength. No person is always right. A leader can never teach others if he or she is not willing to be taught.

SUBMISSIVE AUTHORITY
The Living Free ministry in a local church or ministry is subject to the leadership of the local organization. Living Free is not designed to be done by "freelancers" who are not subject to a structured spiritual authority. Facilitators of groups must be willing to come under the authority of the sponsoring organization.

PREPAREDNESS
People who come to the groups expect the facilitators to be prepared to lead. This includes prayer preparation, knowledge of the Bible passages being studied, and a willingness to devote full attention to the group. For a leader to be unprepared and to fail to "do his homework" is a sure predictor of failure just ahead.

—Thanks to Dr. Terry Lewis for assistance.

Skills and Duties of Great Facilitators

A facilitator does not have to be an expert.

Almost anyone can facilitate a Living Free group if they have a heart for people. The essential qualities of a good facilitator are a servant's heart, emotional stability, and a commitment to becoming like Christ in attitude and behavior. A facilitator does not have to have all of the answers. He or she is there to share, not preach.

A facilitator needs certain qualities and skills to be effective.

A FACILITATOR SHOULD . . .

- Learn by participating in a group.
- Arrive before the group participants.
- Open the meetings with prayer.
- Ask questions.
- Listen actively. Reflect back to the person what you perceive he or she is saying.
- Keep the group focused and on time.
- Share his or her own feelings and experiences at appropriate moments.
- Keep Christ at the center of the group.
- Set a tone that balances sensitivity and humor.
- Keep the group on the topic; avoid "rabbit trails."
- Establish an atmosphere of warmth and trust where the Holy Spirit is free to work in people's lives. Help members know that there is trust and confidentiality within the body of Christ.
- Use yes-or-no questions to help quiet people feel comfortable about responding.
- Place the over-talkers out of eye contact. The more eye contact you have with a talkative person, the more it encourages him or her to talk. Place the talkers beside you.
- Facilitate—keep the process going.
- Care-front with respect and sensitivity.
- Respect each group member's comfort level.
- Create the opportunity for openness.
- Arrange the chairs so members can easily see each other (a circle is best).

A FACILITATOR SHOULD NOT . . .

- Do most of the talking.
- Answer most of the questions.
- Dominate the group in any way.
- Cut a person off while he or she is speaking.
- Be so focused on one person that you lose the attention of other group members.
- Make judgments or give opinions.
- Expect everyone to be comfortable about sharing right away or to have the same level of openness that others have.
- Assume that a quiet person isn't getting anything out of the group. He or she may be taking in everything you say.
- Do group therapy (open up deep wounds).

- Interpret what group members say; instead, reflect what they say.
- Be a "caretaker."
- Be a "know-it-all."
- Permit gossip during the group.
- Be afraid of silence.
- Give advice.
- Neglect to pray regularly for each group member.

Facilitators must know their limitations.

Facilitators are laypersons, not professional clinicians. They need to know when to refer a person to a professional. People using alcohol or other drugs, people with mental illnesses, those who are a danger to themselves or others, and those with other major issues in their lives may need to be referred to a pastor, social worker, counselor, or other professional. Churches should put together a list of resource people and agencies for referral.

Living Free is not a substitute for medical or psychological care. We never advise anyone to stop taking medication or cancel their doctor's care.

We give our time, compassion, and love solely as caring people who want to be channels of Christ's love to those who are hurting and desire wholeness in Christ. As non-credentialed persons, we promise no professional psychological expertise.

Essential Skills for Facilitators to Develop

Avoid being the center of attention.

The most common temptation of a leader is to talk the group to death, to dominate it, to explain, and to answer most of the questions, i.e., to be the "super Christian." This temptation will be aided by the more immature members, who may be dependent upon authoritative figures. These individuals will try to rely on others for the answers instead of thinking for themselves. Any discussion that lasts too long between a leader and an individual loses the rest of the group. Avoid the temptation of feeling that the leader is superior—spiritually or otherwise. Ideally, the function of the leader is to start the discussion, give it direction, and thereafter to simply keep the discussion personal and on track.

Manage the time wisely.

Keep the group on schedule with the different segments, but allow flexibility for people to respond to God. Begin and end the session on time, always allowing time at the end for prayer. People need to be able to count on you that the group will end on time. If they are held over, they may not return. If it is plain that you will need more time because someone in the group is sharing and needs additional time for ministry, be sure to officially dismiss the group on time and invite members who can stay longer to do so.

Keep the group focused on Christ and not on past failures and pain.

It is okay to explain how the past has impacted our lives, but if the group is allowed to dwell there, the members tend to wallow in their misery and lose sight of how they can respond to God in the present.

Guard the comfort level of group members.

Although it does not happen often, someone may begin to disclose too many graphic details of his or her life to the group. If you are uncomfortable with the direction the person is going, gently interrupt the person and help him or her understand that some issues are best discussed in a private session with a minister or other trained person.

We recommend that most groups include both men and women. In these settings, when someone is disclosing sexual sin, we suggest that the person not disclose details beyond the simple fact that they are struggling with sexual purity or a personal problem.

Protect members from those who want to play "therapist."

Learn to head off members who "interrogate" other members by asking them too many questions. Take charge of the group when any one member is giving advice to another or is trying to interpret what is being said. Don't let anyone probe other members for details of a painful experience.

If someone in the group starts to probe, say to that person something like, "Let's let Bill tell it the way he sees it" or "Why don't we give Bill a chance to finish what he has to say?" Each person shares only what he or she freely chooses to say—and no more.

Steer the group away from controversial subjects.

Keep the group on subject, and avoid controversial discussions such as politics, personalities, and doctrinal disputes. These will only waste group time and divert attention from the real issues. Some members will use controversy to avoid dealing with their own problems.

Learn to listen.

Listen with your ears (hear what is being said), with your eyes (be attentive to the one speaking), and with your heart (respond with appropriate emotion). Give each person sharing your undivided attention. Don't worry about what you are going to say—just be there in the moment, and trust God to work. Give verbal responses to what people say and nonverbal responses to let them know you are there with them.

Set good boundaries, and take care of yourself.

Don't "take care of" group members; let them solve their own problems. If you begin to try to solve problems of group members, you will eventually burn yourself out. Be aware that codependency is a real trap for some facilitators.

▶ *If you begin to feel stressed, talk to your minister and Core Team members.*

Challenges and Techniques of Group Communication

Communication in a group is a complex matter. Complexities rise with the number of persons involved. Communication is verbal and nonverbal; it conveys feelings, ideas, hopes, opinions, judgments, and anticipations. Good communication requires the ability to listen and to enter into the experiences of others. A good communicator is able to capably express his or her ideas and feelings to others. Skill in communication requires practice. Often old patterns need to be broken so that new patterns of listening and speaking can be learned.

Discussions are better facilitated when a leader asks a question and looks around the group until someone answers. The leader then asks, "What did others find?" or "What facts did someone else discover?" The leader watches for someone who wants to speak rather than pointing out a specific individual.

When a leader patiently persists with good guiding questions, the members will begin addressing their replies to the group and the group grows from leader centered to group centered.

Seldom answer your own question: Direct queries to the group and wait! If no one responds, then rephrase the question, or just wait it out. Don't be afraid of silence. Make the group dig for answers. Don't let your insecurity about silent moments ruin God's dialogue with members of the group.

When a leader continually directs questions to specific individuals, it may embarrass those persons if they do not have an answer. Directing questions to individuals can result in the group's becoming dependent on the leader to conduct a series of conversations. Any discussion that lasts too long between a leader and an individual loses the rest of the group.

Facilitation of sharing in a group may entail quieting the compulsive talker and bringing the silent person into the discussion. The first step in quieting an overly talkative person is to stop encouraging his or her behavior. This can be done by breaking eye contact with the speaker and by not nodding your head. Eye contact and nodding the head encourage him or her to keep talking. If this does not work, the next step is to divert the conversation away from the person by means of a question or statement, like "Perhaps someone else would like to share what they have discovered about this"; "While we are on this point, let's hear from some of the others"; "Can we save your other points until later?"; or "You've raised a number of interesting points that should keep us busy a good while. Would anyone else like to comment on them?" If all your "hints" are not successful, you may need to speak with the person privately.

Seating arrangements affect communication: People who sit across from each other speak more to each other than do people sitting next to each other. Make sure everyone can see everyone else. A circle of chairs is best, and eye contact is a must.

Stages of Progression for Some Common Problems

Stages of Progression for Eating Disorders

PHASE ONE: EXPERIMENTATION

No one starts a diet with the intention of becoming anorexic, yet dieting is how all anorexics start out. In the same way, no one who decides to control his or her weight by vomiting, laxative use, or any other forms of purging ever believes that he or she will end up in an out-of-control cycle of binging and purging. In fact, eating disorders generally start out as a way of being in control—in control of food, weight, one's size, or one's image.

PHASE TWO: SOCIAL USE

Our society's norms have a profound influence on the development of anorexic or bulimic tendencies. Social norms for attractiveness modeled in magazines, movies, and television have pressed the image of fitness into a slender shape ideal.

The health benefits of exercise are promoted and distorted as weight-loss strategies. Peer pressure triggers and reinforces the obsessive drive for thinness in individuals prone to an eating disorder. Friends often play a role in the development of each other's eating disorders by teaching each other that if you throw up or don't eat, you will not gain weight.

PHASE THREE: DAILY PREOCCUPATION

For the person who is becoming anorexic, dieting and losing weight quickly take on a function that is unanticipated and unplanned. As the person begins to lose weight, he or she feels a new-found control over life where he or she had previously felt ineffective or weak. Suddenly there is a feeling of power—a feeling that gradually controls every area of daily functioning.

Initial attempts to overcome feelings of incompetence, unworthiness, and ineffectiveness are replaced with preoccupation and symbolic control. Eventually, food ceases to serve a physical function and begins to serve psychological functions.

PHASE FOUR: PRACTICING/USING JUST TO FEEL NORMAL

Restrictive eating leads to distorted sight; the anorexic truly sees an inaccurate body image in the mirror. Any attempt to choose to eat normally is pre-empted by the fear of "not being able to stop." And so the anorexic loses control and becomes obsessed with how many calories have been consumed, how many he or she has burned, and how to place more and more restrictions on this area he or she has so much "control" over.

For the bulimic, the purge is the antidote to loss of control over food. A bulimic thinks, "When I binge, I lose. When I purge, the food loses."

What started out as an attempt to control body weight has become a behavior that is out of control. Initially, turning to food actually works to make the bulimic feel calmer and less under pressure. The more effective this method is, the more entrenched the behavior becomes as a way of coping with uncomfortable emotional states. Soon, the bulimic thinks more and more about eating and purging.

She or he begins to structure the day around when and what to eat, and how to get rid of the calories. The bulimia takes on a life of its own, and the person no longer feels a choice to binge or vomit—the binge/purge cycle has taken over his or her life.

—Thanks to Martha Homme

Stages of Progression in Sexual Addiction

Patrick Carnes, in his book *Out of the Shadows*, describes the **sexual-addiction** cycle (9).

For sexual addictions, an addictive experience progresses through a four-step cycle that intensifies with each repetition.

PHASE ONE: PREOCCUPATION
The trance or mood wherein the addict's mind is completely engrossed with thoughts of sex. This mental state creates an obsessive search for sexual stimulation.

PHASE TWO: RITUALIZATION
The addict's own special routines that lead up to the sexual behavior. The ritual intensifies the preoccupation, adding arousal and excitement.

PHASE THREE: COMPULSIVE SEXUAL BEHAVIOR
The actual sexual act, which is the end goal of the preoccupation and ritualization. Sexual addicts are unable to control or stop this behavior.

PHASE FOUR: DESPAIR
The feeling of utter hopelessness addicts have about their behavior and their powerlessness.

Stages of Progression for Fear

Our *Living Free* DVD segment mentioned that the root of many life-controlling problems is fear. Below are the phases of the development of fear and anger.

PHASE ONE: STRESS
Any cause of stress in life can become overwhelming—people, places, or things.

PHASE TWO: ANXIETY
This is a feeling of reaction to the stressor.

PHASE THREE: AVOIDANCE
Often people avoid confronting the cause of stress, and bitterness begins. Unforgiveness is also an avoidance technique. All forms of avoidance isolate the individual.

PHASE FOUR: REINFORCEMENT
After repeated avoidance of confronting the anxiety or stress, avoidance behaviors are reinforced. Continued reinforcement causes the problem to persist.

Instead of avoiding an issue, deal with the anxiety and reverse the cycle of fear.

Confrontation allows resolution of the anxiety.

Stages of Progression for Anger

There are seven phases involved with anger.

PHASE ONE: HURT
The person experiences bruised feelings from a personal slight or disappointment.

PHASE TWO: FRUSTRATION
This is the feeling that comes when life tells you no.

PHASE THREE: FEAR
When we experience loss of control or anticipation of reprisal, fear sets in.

PHASE FOUR: ANGER
When a perception of hurt is complicated by frustration and fear, it becomes anger.

PHASE FIVE: WRATH
Anger that has brewed overnight and become mixed with bitterness and unforgiveness is wrath.

PHASE SIX: HOSTILITY
When wrath has collected and turns aggressive, it becomes hostility.

PHASE SEVEN: HATE
Bottled-up hostility with thoughts of aggression toward a person, group, or object—possibly leading to murder, suicide, or depression—is hate.

In order to deal with anger, go back to the hurt, acknowledge it, and take responsibility for your part while forgiving the other person for his or her part.

—Thanks to Dr. Raymond Brock

Idols Are God-Substitutes

A stronghold becomes an idol in our lives when it diverts our attention from our relationship with Christ.

We begin to trust the idol to help us cope with life, and the idol eventually becomes a substitute for a relationship with God. The second commandment found in God's Word, the Bible, says: "You shall not make for yourself an idol in the form of anything in heaven above on the earth beneath or in the waters below. You shall not bow down to them or worship them; for I, the LORD your God, am a jealous God" (Exodus 20:4-5).

Anything that we substitute for God is an idol. Jeffrey Van Vonderen, in his book *Good News for the Chemically Dependent*, defines an idol as:

> Anything besides God to which we turn, positive or negative, in order to find life, value, and meaning is idolatry: Money, property, jewels, sex, clothes, church buildings, educational degrees, anything! Because of Christ's performance on the cross, life, value, and purpose are available to us in gift form only. Anything we do, positive or negative, to earn that which is life by our own performance is idolatrous: robbing a bank, cheating on our spouse, people-pleasing, swindling our employer, attending church, giving 10 percent, playing the organ for twenty years, anything (16)!

Idolatry leads to addiction

When we follow idols, a choice has been made to look to the substance, behavior, or relationship for help that only God can provide. Following an idol will prevent us from serving and loving God freely. Idols only add baggage to our lives and weigh us down. As the prophet Jeremiah states, "They must be carried because they cannot walk" (Jeremiah 10:5).

John Stott gives a clear comparison between idols and God:

> For idols are dead; God is living. Idols are false; God is true. Idols are many; God is one. Idols are visible and tangible; God is invisible and intangible, beyond the reach of sight and touch. Idols are creatures, the work of human hands; God is the Creator of the universe and of all humankind. . . . And the more sophisticated idols (that is, God-substitutes) of modern secular cities

are equally powerful. Some people are eaten up with a selfish ambition for money, power, or fame. Others are obsessed with their work, or with sport or television, or are infatuated with a person, or addicted to food, alcohol, hard drugs, or sex. Both immorality and greed are later pronounced by Paul to be forms of idolatry because they demand an allegiance which is due to God alone. So every idolater is a prisoner, held in humiliating bondage (39).

Plan of Salvation

How to receive Christ:

1. Admit your need (that you are a sinner).

2. Be willing to turn from your sins (repent).

3. Believe that Jesus Christ died for you on the cross and rose from the grave.

4. Through prayer, invite Jesus Christ to come in and control your life through the Holy Spirit (receive Him as Savior and Lord).

What to Pray

Dear God,
I know that I am a sinner and need Your forgiveness.
I believe that Jesus Christ died for my sins.
I am willing to turn from my sins.
I now invite Jesus Christ to come into my heart and life as my personal Savior.
I am willing, by God's strength, to follow and obey Jesus Christ as the Lord of my life.

_____
Date   Signature

The Bible says: "Everyone who calls on the name of the Lord will be saved" (*Romans 10:13*).

"Yet to all who received him, to those who believed in his name, he gave the right to become children of God" (*John 1:12*).

"Therefore, since we have been justified through faith, we have peace with God through our Lord Jesus Christ" (*Romans 5:1*).

When we receive Christ, we are born into the family of God through the supernatural work of the Holy Spirit, who lives within every believer. This process is called regeneration or the new birth.

Share your decision to receive Christ with another person.

Connect to a local church.

References

Augsburger, David. *Caring Enough to Confront*. Glendale: Regal, 1980.

Balswick, Jack O., and Judith K Blaswick. *The Family: A Christian Perspective on the Contemporary Home*. Grand Rapids: Baker, 1989.

Beattie, Melody. *Codependent No More*. New York: Harper & Row, 1988.

Black, Claudia. *It Will Never Happen to Me*. New York: Ballantine Books, 1981.

Capell-Sowder, Kathy, et al. *Codependency: An Emerging Issue*. Pompano Beach: Health Communications, 1984.

Crabb, Lawrence J. *Effective Biblical Counseling*. Grand Rapids: Zondervan, 1977.

Crowley, James F. Community Intervention. Minneapolis: Community Intervention, 1981.

Hart, Archibald D. *Counseling the Depressed*. Dallas: Word Publishing, 1987.

Hersh, Sharon A. *The Last Addiction*. Colorado Springs: WaterBrook Press, 2008.

Holwerda, Jim and David Egner. "Doing Away with Addiction." Discovery Digest, Vol. 12, No. 4, Grand Rapids: Radio Bible Class, 1988.

Johnson, Vernon E. *I'll Quit Tomorrow*. San Francisco: Harper & Row, 1980.

Krupnick, Louis B., and Elizabeth Krupnick. *From Despair to Decision*. Minneapolis: CompCare Publications, 1985.

Kubler-Ross, Elisabeth. *On Death and Dying*. New York: MacMillan, 1970.

Lean, Garth. *On the Tail of a Comet*. Colorado Springs: Helmers and Howard, 1985.

Lee, Jimmy Ray. *Living Free Instructor's Guide*. Chattanooga: Living Free, 1988.

Lee, Jimmy Ray. *Understanding the Times and Knowing What to Do*. Chattanooga, TN: Living Free, 1997.

Leerhsen, Charles, and Tessa Namuth. "Alcohol and the Family." Newsweek, CXI, 18 January 1988, pp. 62-68.

Luft, Joseph. *Group Processes: An Introduction to Group Dynamics*. Mountain View, CA: Mayfield Publishing Co., 1984.

Meier, Paul D., Donald E. Ratcliff, and Frederick L. Rowe. *Child-Rearing*. Grand Rapids: Baker, 1993.

Menninger, Karl. *Whatever Became of Sin?* New York: Hawthorne, 1973.

Miller, J. Keith. *Sin: Overcoming the Ultimate Deadly Addiction*. San Francisco: Harper & Row, 1987.

Minrith, Frank, Paul Meier, Siegfried Fink, Walter Byrd, and Don Hawkins. *Taking Control*. Grand Rapids: Baker Book House, 1988.

Murphy, John Robin. *Be Transformed*. Brentwood, TN: Rock House Way Press, LLC, 2007.

Pearlman, Myer. *Daniel Speaks Today*. Springfield: Gospel Publishing House, 1943.

Perkins, Bill. *Fatal Attractions*. Eugene: Harvest House, 1991.

Smalley, Gary. *For Better or For Best*. Grand Rapids: Zondervan, 1988.

Sowder-Capell, Kathy and Others. *Co-Dependency: An Emerging Issue*. Pompano Beach: Health Communications, 1984.

Stanley, Charles F. *Handle with Care*. Wheaton: Victor, 1988.

Stott, John. *The Gospel and the End of Time*. Downers Grove: InterVarsity, 1991.

Sweeten, Gary. *Apples of Gold I*. Cincinnati: Christian Information Committee, 1983.

Sweeten, Gary. *Apples of Gold II Teacher's Manual*. Cincinnati: Christian Information Committee, 1983.

Turnbull, Ralph G., ed. *Baker's Handbook of Practical Theology*. Grand Rapids: Baker Book House, 1967.

VanVonderen, Jeffery. *Good News for the Chemically Dependent*. Nashville: Thomas Nelson, 1985.

Wegscheider, Sharon. "Children of Alcoholics Caught in Family Trap." Focus on Alcohol and Drugs Issues 2, May-June, 1979.